BEETHOVEN'S
PIANOFORTE SONATAS

AMS PRESS
NEW YORK

Louis Van Beethoven

Frontispiece

LUDWIG van BEETHOVEN'S
PIANOFORTE SONATAS

BY
WILLIAM BEHREND

TRANSLATED FROM THE DANISH BY
INGEBORG LUND

INTRODUCTION BY
ALFRED CORTOT

*With Twenty-three Illustrations in Half-Tone
and numerous Examples of his Music*

MCMXXVII
LONDON & TORONTO
J. M. DENT & SONS LTD.
NEW YORK: E. P. DUTTON & CO.

Library of Congress Cataloging in Publication Data

Behrend, William 1861-1940.
    Ludwig van Beethoven's pianoforte sonatas.

    Reprint of the 1927 ed. published by J. M. Dent, London
and E. P. Dutton, New York.
    Original t.p.: Translated from the Danish by Ingeborg
Lund; introd. by Alfred Cortot; with 23 illus. in
half-tone and numerous examples of his music.
    Includes index.
    1. Beethoven, Ludwig van, 1770-1827. Sonatas, piano.
I. Title.
ML410.B42B45 1978   786.4'1'54   74-24038
ISBN 0-404-12861-0

Reprinted from the edition of 1927, London and New York
First AMS edition published in 1978
Manufactured in the United States of America

AMS PRESS INC.
NEW YORK, N.Y.

INTRODUCTION

BEETHOVEN'S SONATAS have been for nearly half a
century the subject of a whole series of critical editions
and technical commentaries of the greatest interest,
but of which the incontestable merits are counter-
balanced by a tiresome defect. This is that they
have quite certainly altered, not, perhaps, the musical
significance of these incomparable piano poems, but
at least the state of emotional receptivity in which one
ought to approach them. The nuances have been
indicated, the fingering marked, the pauses timed, the
ties examined, the accents explained—and, perhaps,
the true spirit has been neglected.

Analysis has been applied to everything except to
that which gave to these great masterpieces the
character of an immortal confession ; the confession of
a melancholy and lonely being, who all his life long—
from childhood till the day of his death, or near it—
confided daily to his instrument his most secret
meditations, the bitterness of his torments, his revolts,
his unattainable hopes ; the confession of a soul who,
in Liszt's phrase, " *avait mal à l'humanité.*" That
mighty urge of love or indignation which gave wings to
his sublime thought, which alone ordered his flight
and limited his horizon, we have sometimes been

tempted to forget, under the weight of so much contradictory guidance and so many theoretical explanations.

This remarkable work by William Behrend comes at the right moment in the centenary year when we piously endeavour to revive in our own imagination the true mind of the musician " trained in the school of misfortune."

While it remains entirely personal, it is not without analogy to the generous essay by Lenz on Beethoven and his three styles ; and, like that work, it sets out to interpret the reasons for Beethoven's inspiration rather than the necessities of form, the beauty of his music rather than the difficulties of the instrument.

Certainly a work of this kind can only be based on hypothesis, and when it concerns Beethoven, who said —at least if Schindler is to be believed—" They " (meaning us, the public, the musicians, the virtuosi) " would be terrified if they knew what I am thinking when I compose "—then hypothesis can carry us far.

Be that as it may, the point cannot be over-emphasised that of all the interpretations suggested by the reading of William Behrend's book, there is not a single one which does not tend to the noblest conception. Further, the author, wherever possible, supports his theories by the most carefully chosen and convincing documentary evidence. And rediscovering the man behind the work, he makes it possible for us to dream the work anew beyond the man thus revealed. This is what true interpretation means.

Thanks are due to William Behrend for pulling us up so sharply—for restoring to the living work its pathetic power, its compelling savour. Even if one does not always share his feeling (and particularly in what concerns sonatas 81, 110, and 111, we ought never to forget the eloquent and searching commentaries of a d'Indy or a Taine), we can nevertheless follow him confidently. By safe roads he leads us to meet the great, the true, the only Beethoven.

ALFRED CORTOT.

Paris, January 1927.

PREFACE TO THE
FIRST DANISH EDITION

This book owes its origin to a course of lectures which I gave a few years ago at the Royal Danish Conservatoire of Music, on the greater number of Beethoven's Sonatas for Piano (up to Opus 81). The lectures were intended to be a kind of historical, biographical and psychological supplement to the practical teaching of the sonatas ; this origin gives something of the point of view of the book. I took up the task again later, urged partly by the need of bringing the consideration of the sonatas to a close; partly by the desire to produce such a work just when a century had elapsed since the publication of the last Beethoven sonata for piano. My efforts were then directed, in extending and elaborating the material, towards producing a book for " Everyman," which could be read by every lover of music, by everyone who is a performer, or who hears Beethoven's sonatas performed in the concert-room or at home, or who is in any way attracted by his music and his personality—a book which could be read without much previous knowledge of the subject, not only for the sake of learning but for that of entertainment. In the introductory chapter I have tried to communicate to the reader the more particular object of the book. I will only add that if it has partly become a Beethoven biography *in nuce*, this is not quite beyond my intention, and I shall regret it the less if it can lead the reader on to a closer study of the great biographies, the collections of letters and the like, concerning this remarkable genius and artist.

W. B.

1923.

BEETHOVEN (*c.* 1803).
(*From a miniature by Christian Horneman.*)

PREFACE TO THE
SECOND DANISH EDITION

AFTER barely four months it was already necessary to prepare a new edition of the present book. It was in the main only a question of reprinting—yet so that certain desirable or necessary improvements were carried out, and it seemed to me that I might feel justified in restricting myself to this with all the better reason because of the reception accorded to my book in reviews, several of which were written over the best names in our musical world, and which did not contain objections or recommendations of any importance.

As encroachments on the text or additions to it have thus been avoided, I may perhaps venture to make two remarks here which would otherwise belong to Chapters VI and XVII of the book. Concerning Opus 27, No. II (C sharp minor), Edwin Fischer has drawn my attention to a resemblance between the beginning of the Adagio and a famous passage in the first act of Mozart's *Don Giovanni* (after the murder of the Commandant), and pointed out that Beethoven himself had copied out this passage. I have not been able to obtain further knowledge on this matter, but there can hardly be any doubt about the impression made on Beethoven by that inspired passage. He may, therefore, have been influenced, but this need not imply any imitation or actual resemblance. (Concerning the latter, see further p. 52 and the matter dealt with there.) With regard to Opus 110 (A flat), I have been struck by a certain resemblance between the Fugue in the Finale and a Fugue by A. Scarlatti (C minor—F major) edited by Louis Köhler (amongst

others) in *Les Maîtres du Clavecin*, Vol. II, Litolff's edition.
Although Scarlatti's music for piano must for many reasons be
supposed to have been well known to Beethoven, I did not
venture to make any observations about a resemblance which
is more concerned with character and attitude in general than
with ostensible melodic or other identities which might also
be accidental.   After my book had been issued, however, I
received from Professor Dr. Buhl an inquiry as to whether I
had not noticed the resemblance between the two fugues.
It seems to me, then, that I ought to point it out here, since it
does not depend on an individual opinion, and so much the
more, as it seems at any rate to strengthen the remark on
p. 182, that it is more likely to have been the fugue-works
of Händel (under Italian influence) that were present to
Beethoven's mind.

W. B.

April 1924.

LIST OF ILLUSTRATIONS

" Les sonates de Beethoven sont peut-être plus intéressantes que des compositions d'un genre techniquement supérieur, en ce sens qu'elles nous offrent un document psychologique de premier ordre."—COMBARIEU.

BEETHOVEN'S
PIANOFORTE SONATAS

CHAPTER I

THE *Wohltemperiertes Clavier* of Johann Sebastian Bach and
the *Sonatas for Piano* of Ludwig van Beethoven have been called
the Old and New Testament of the piano, and it has been said
that though all music were to perish and only these two works
to survive, a sufficient knowledge of the music of the eighteenth
and nineteenth centuries could be obtained from them alone.
Students in a distant future will always be able to gain from
them a clear perception of the musical ideas and modes of
expression of the periods to which each of them belongs. These
two works reveal the grandeur of the two minds from which
they sprang, and testify to the character of the genius that
inspired them. They stand side by side as the types of an
older and newer age, as the representatives of two periods of art.

Otherwise the contrast between the two works is at once
evident. Bach's double series of preludes and fugues, however
clearly bearing the stamp of genius in their variety and wealth
of invention, show in the main one common physiognomy,
the expression of which varies within certain limits. It is a
well-known fact that the *Wohltemperiertes Clavier* appeared
in two volumes at an interval of twenty years, yet each of the
two volumes was—or might well have been—written in one
continuous series within a comparatively short space of time.
Beethoven's sonatas, on the other hand, extend over the whole

B

of his life, from his boyhood to the last years of his manhood. They bear the impress of this. In their purely exterior form they differ widely. If Bach in his *Wohltemperiertes Clavier* reached two high-water marks in his compositions for the piano, Beethoven in his sonatas gives an account of his whole life in its changing phases. It is the life of a genius, and therefore beyond our horizon, yet it is so humanly near our understanding that we can contemplate with sympathy its development and varying destiny. We can, as it were, follow the life of the Master through his sonatas, sometimes almost from one sonata to another; and as no two of them are alike, either in form or in theme, this is all the more easily done.

A Beethoven sonata, then, is not only a beautiful and artistic piece of music, a source of enjoyment to those who listen to it, and an education to those who perform it; it is, with few exceptions, an independent and individual revelation of the composer's genius, giving an insight into his spiritual life and his experiences. In the piano sonatas, especially, one is justified in looking for instances of these intimate self-revelations, as the piano was his favourite instrument, the only one that he mastered to perfection and to which he confided his deepest secrets. If we consider the violin sonatas, for instance, which in their outward construction differ very little from those written for the piano, they seem to us, taking them altogether, not quite so tenderly self-revealing as the latter. However refined they are as works of art, however beautiful and rich in expression are sonatas like that dedicated to Kreutzer and the two in G major—to mention outstanding examples—they seem, more than the greater number of the piano sonatas, to indicate a " social " purpose, that is, that they had been composed for the entertainment of an audience gathered together with that object in view. The piano as a solo instrument is the Master's medium of expression in his solitude, though in varying degrees, throughout the series of sonatas. In them he plays to us in such a way that often, in quiet consecrated moments, we seem to come very close to his heart and to enjoy his confidence, without having our thoughts diverted to other objects. Nor can it be a mere accident that the series of violin sonatas ceases at Opus 96, at a time when Beethoven, then about forty years old, had not withdrawn from the world, but felt attracted by it, and bound to it by the social ties of friends and benefactors; whereas the piano sonatas are continued up to Opus 111, that is to say, far further into his years of loneliness, in fact till close up to the time of his death.

It is only natural, on the other hand, that this intimate spirit is not found in the piano *concertos* in the same degree as in the sonatas. The concertos were written for the greater world, the world that visits concert-rooms, or, as they were called in those days, "the Academies." The demand for executive brilliance is strongly emphasised, yet in a noble sense; external splendour is a conscious object of the music in another way and in a higher degree than in the sonatas; the voice of the orchestra tends to produce greater realism than when the piano is speaking alone; the frequently larger plan and more accessible and open construction lead away from the intimate and the freer play of tone in the sonatas.

Now if we consider this long series of piano sonatas as a deeply felt and spontaneous utterance of Beethoven's personality during the changing conditions of his life, we shall find that they possess a deeper significance and interest, both individually and as a whole. It is not mainly because one sonata is more "difficult" than another that it occupies its particular place in the series. It is because the composer was one man when he wrote, for instance, the "Waldstein" sonata, and another, both in a spiritual and in a musically technical sense—as a composer and a pianist—when he wrote the so-called "Pathétique." Nor could he possibly have written the great "Hammerklavier" sonata before that which is known as the "Moonlight" sonata. When all this becomes clear to us, the sonatas will be filled with deeper meanings and be of more value than if we contemplate any individual sonata merely according to its importance as a masterpiece for the piano.

Meanwhile our present object is not that of studying the sonatas from the last-mentioned point of view. That would lead us beyond the scope of this book and into that of text-books on theory and analysis. Our purpose is rather to dwell on that with which practical teaching is but slightly concerned, the human, personal element in Beethoven's sonatas—thus, to which part of his life each sonata belongs, under what conditions it came into being, what connection it may have had with events in his life and the like; what can be traced through dedications and by other means about the value and importance of the sonata to the composer; and further, what we can learn in various ways through the sonata about the interior life of the Master, the decisive events in his life, his character, his artistic ideals, and so forth. In the end the sonatas themselves will reveal all this to us, and in the following pages we shall mainly be engaged in studying their themes. But in order to throw as strong and vivid a light as possible on this music, we will try to gather together the material from which we can arrive at a clearer understanding of the com-poser and his work. To many modern students of the piano Beethoven is perhaps only a composer who has written these often very "difficult" sonatas, and the only thing to be done with them is to practise them again and again. It is hoped that in these pages the composer of the sonatas may become, both to the performer and the listener, a living man, greater, grander than his fellows, one who has felt, thought, dreamed, fought and suffered more than we, who has, in fact, "suffered for us." It is by no means a bad method, when studying a work of art, whether it be a poem, a drama, a picture or a piece of music, to try to perceive and understand the personality of the man standing behind it as its creator.   In any case one is certain of deriving great profit from this method.

*   *   *   *   *   *

Beethoven wrote his first piano sonata when he was about twelve years old.   He wrote his last when he was fifty-two, five years before he died.   We can, therefore, follow him in the sonatas through forty years of his life, and realise with Walter Niemann, in his *Klavierbuch*, that " The development of Beethoven's piano music, its gradual changes and the composer's energetic attempts to find new forms, can be fully understood only by those who continually try to trace the intimate co-operation between the artist and the man."

CHAPTER II

LUDWIG VAN BEETHOVEN was born in Bonn in 1770, and, as everyone knows, he was destined from his childhood by a drunken and somewhat brutal father to be an infant prodigy, after the pattern furnished not many years earlier by the brilliant career of Wolfgang Mozart; but unfortunately Beethoven's father was not a Leopold Mozart, either as a man or a musician. He can hardly have understood, like the latter, the rare gifts of his son, and in any case he was incapable of developing them, or of educating the boy, and humanly speaking giving him a serious training and a proper understanding of his future.* It was, in fact, a rather rough school in which this boy was taught by his father and Thomas Pfeiffer, his father's boon companion. Nevertheless, the boy at an early age attained to fluency in playing the piano and to composing small pieces for his instrument. He created a stir in Bonn, this being further aided by the efforts of his father in persistent and not always honest advertisement.

He was not put under artistic care and training until he was twelve years old, when Christian Gottlieb Neefe became his teacher. This physically deformed musician was a gifted composer and æsthete, also a writer, and probably for the first time his young pupil received a deeper insight into music as an art. In after years Beethoven acknowledged Neefe's influence on his development, and this not merely as regards technique and theory. Moreover, Neefe was a modern musician in his day; he followed in the footsteps of Philip Emmanuel Bach,

* In *Der junge Beethoven* Professor L. Schiedermair has made a well-meant attempt at softening the portrait of Beethoven's father, yet without *essentially* altering it.

CHRISTIAN GOTTLIEB NEEFE.

with those who had emancipated themselves from the strict polyphonic style of earlier times; who aimed at a freer, more definite and more deeply felt form of musical expression, and were in favour with the art-patrons of the day, the "Liebhaber," as they were called. But Neefe had been trained in the serious-minded North German school, and it was perhaps not accidental—though it may have been chiefly for educational reasons—that he made his pupil practise Sebastian Bach's *Wohltemperiertes Clavier* so diligently that even when he was quite young he could play many of these preludes and fugues by heart. Later on, when he came to Vienna in 1792, he had to play such pieces as these to one of his aristocratic patrons, the aged Baron von Swieten, as a sort of "Evening Benediction." This would most likely be when the less intimate guests had left, while the more cultivated "connoisseurs," worshippers of good, old music, stayed behind and needed serious evening devotions after the more or less empty virtuoso music to which they had listened in the course of the evening. For the ears of Viennese society were pleasantly tickled by what would now be called "drawing-room" music, which had caused such inflammation in them that for a long time they could not appreciate the overwhelming difference between this music and that produced by the young Beethoven.

Yet we should perhaps scarcely be right in saying that Beethoven's attitude to Sebastian Bach's music at this time was particularly sympathetic or appreciative. He was undoubtedly deeply impressed by its infinite wealth and invention in a musically technical sense, but apart from this he was drawn in another direction. This Bach music, which had originally been taught him in the form of exercises, must have been in his mind when later on (in Vienna) he speaks of "the old forms handed down, to which it must be our object at the present day to add a really poetic element." At Bonn the young musician would also come into contact with other movements of the day which attracted general attention. One of these was the music of the so-called " Mannheim school," which had a following in Bonn. Here his highly gifted and watchful spirit heard an interpretation that again was far removed from that of Sebastian Bach, a brisk, piquant, one might almost say dashing, mode of playing with a varied accentuation. It was influenced by the Italian school and by the southern temperament—in contrast to the drier and more scholarly music language of North Germany—and found expression in a vivacious orchestra with shadings and dynamic effects hitherto unknown—at any rate as a principle. In these and the singing *allegro* there was an endeavour to make the new sonata form a supple, impassioned means of expression for two themes of contrasting ideas and moods, in orchestral and chamber music, such as it was in the hands of Philip Emmanuel Bach at the piano. Thus the heralding of what Haydn and Mozart were soon to develop and enrich, and raise to a higher spiritual sphere, was heard by Beethoven in his childhood at Bonn. Hugo Riemann, in particular, has pointed out evidence of his Mannheim sympathies in his older works, but whether or not his tutor, Neefe, guided by his own sterner training, warned his pupil against these tendencies, can hardly now be ascertained. There can be no doubt, however, that his growing genius was considerably influenced by a variety of tendencies in music.

Like all musical minds in the last decades of the eighteenth century, Beethoven would also be captivated by that new form, the sonata. It was discovered that here was a new means of creating musical pieces of a strangely life-like character, of richly varied themes and great perspicuity; they were, in fact, small but entire musical organisms.

The oft-quoted exclamation of the poet and æsthete, Fontenelle: " Sonate, que me veux-tu ? " was probably in the first instance a question directed to a form of music that spoke to its listeners naked, not clothed in words, in contrast to operatic music; but it also contains a hesitating fear in the presence of something new that has found expression in music. They did not quite understand it as yet, but instinctively it was felt to be the dawn of a significant mode of expressing, by means of musical sounds, the varying moods and feelings of the human soul. In reality they were faced by a great gain to music, one which was to show itself possessed of sufficient vital power to endure through generations down to our own time.

The youthful Beethoven must have followed with tense interest the immense progress made by the sonata in the hands of Mozart and Haydn, and it has been proved from history and style how these two composers soon became models for his own productions. At this distance of time it is hardly possible to say definitely when his powers began to stir in him and urge him to independent creative work, not produced in obedience to orders from his father; whether he felt that he was to be the successor of the Vienna masters and to carry on their work. There is no direct proof of this, but that music-loving circles in Bonn took this view of the young musician is shown by their sending him to Vienna to learn of these two masters—though with no great result as regards Mozart. It is shown still more emphatically in the oft-quoted, gravely worded lines on an album leaf, written by Count Ferdinand von Waldstein, one of Beethoven's most eager and able supporters of the Bonn period: " You are now going to Vienna in fulfilment of your long-cherished desire. Mozart's genius is still mourning over the death of her favourite. She has taken refuge with the inexhaustible Haydn, but has not found occupation. If you labour with unwearying diligence you will receive the spirit of Mozart at the hands of Haydn."

*   *   *   *   *   *

The first sonatas,* published in Bonn (1783), bear the title :
" Three sonatas for piano, dedicated to The Most Reverend
The Archbishop and Elector-Prince Maximilian Friedrich, my
most gracious master, and composed by Ludwig van Beethoven,
11 years of age." The last item was one of his father's adver-
tising tricks, as Ludwig was then actually thirteen years old !
The world likes being cheated, and the taste for infant prodigies
(in all branches of music) seems never to change !

The book is provided with a fulsome preface addressed to
the Archbishop, in which the following lines occur : " From my
fourth year music began to be my chief occupation. . . . I
have now already reached my eleventh (?) year, and since then
the muse has often whispered to me in moments of initiation :
' Attempt it, write down the harmonies of thy soul ! ' Eleven
years, I thought, how will the author's mien suit me ? And
what will men in the world of art say to this ? I was almost
on the point of being afraid. Yet—at the bidding of my muse—
I obeyed, and wrote."

This monstrous piece of affectation—which must, of course,
be regarded in the light of the manners of the time—was
fortunately not written by Beethoven himself ; it is believed
to be the work of the " literary " Neefe. The Ludwig who had
composed the sonatas was a little, dark-skinned, pock-marked
fellow, with large, brilliant eyes, but with a shy and reserved
manner ; he sometimes looked untidy and not very clean ; he
could be abrupt and obstinate, and embittered in mind at the
circumstances prevailing at home, which made him both
awkward and lonely. He would hardly have written a preface
like that quoted above, nor perhaps would he have understood
how to fawn like this upon the exalted prince. The publication of the sonatas perhaps earned for him a slight honour and

---

* They are easily accessible in Litolff's edition of Beethoven's sonatas, in which they
are printed as a supplement to the generally known sonatas furnished with *opus*
numbers.

ELEONORE VON BREUNING.

SILHOUETTE OF BEETHOVEN (*c.* 1786).

a badly needed income; perhaps they also—owing to the pompous preface—procured him an advancement. At any rate the boy became a "Court musician" the year after, and we can imagine him dressed in a smart uniform, nay, even wearing a bag-wig.

The sonatas, which were also offered for sale as "an excellent composition by a *genius of eleven years*"—it is no wonder that Beethoven later on in life was sometimes bewildered about his age!—are, of course, only of historical interest, but this they do possess. In the F minor sonata, for instance, indications can be pointed out of something "Beethovenesque" in the form (as in the "Pathétique" sonata with the introductory and recurring *Largo*) and in the choice of key, even though it is difficult to agree with Paul Bekker, who contends that here is a forerunner of the "Appassionata" sonata itself! But this F minor was, and continued to be, the key to which Beethoven had recourse when he had something obscure and passionate to express; consciously or unconsciously, then, he chose it here, where his child's mind was burdened by something, or where his boyish defiance was to be expressed in sound. In the D major sonata an idea suddenly surges up, very like that which many years after (1812) adorns the introduction to the A major symphony. When one knows how Beethoven later on in life carried his ideas in his mind for years, to bring them out, now for this, now for that, treatment, one cannot venture in this instance to speak of a mere chance. Several characteristic passages that now give the impression of a perspective can be pointed out in these childhood sonatas, and more than one phrase in them, more than one melodic idea or pregnant rhythm testify to a depth of feeling and a sense of music that must be called rare even in an unusually advanced and gifted child of thirteen. In one particular sonata movement (G major) one has a feeling that Neefe, the song composer, was the boy's tutor.

There is a small sonata from the Bonn period which for a particular reason deserves closer consideration, although it was not even completed by Beethoven himself (Ferdinand Ries added the conclusion), not exactly for the sake of the music, but because of its connection with the name of a family of great influence on the life of Beethoven. The sonata was intended for Eleonore von Breuning. The house of the widowed Frau von Breuning was one of the wealthy and refined homes in Bonn, and Ludwig van Beethoven was introduced into it as a teacher to the children. He grew so much at home in it that he sometimes spent whole days and nights there, probably when the state of affairs in Rheingasse 934—his own home—was particularly unedifying. In this household the young genius learned refined manners and a cultivated form of intercourse; here more than anywhere else his oddities were understood, and were tolerated because of the spiritual greatness he was felt to possess, when he was in one of his " tantrums " (" Raptus "), as they said amongst themselves. He became a friend of the sons of the house; with one of them, Stephan, the friendship was lifelong, for he also went to Vienna soon after. Stephan's son Gerhard wrote the book, *Aus dem Schwarzpanierhaus*, which contains a valuable description of Beethoven's latter years. Moreover, Beethoven was *probably* not a little enamoured of the dainty and charming Eleonore. We have also other evidence that at this time, about his twentieth year, Beethoven's heart was disturbed by passionate Werther feelings, and it can hardly be doubted that they were concerned with Eleonore Breuning, from the emotional letter of reconciliation that he wrote to her in 1790 (or '91) after a passing quarrel or disagreement. In this letter we get a glimpse for the first time of Beethoven's rugged and independent character, which led so easily to friction between himself and those who only desired his happiness. Another instance can be found in a letter from Vienna (1793) in which he still remembers his friend Eleonore and all the happy days in Bonn. Some time after, Eleonore married Beethoven's friend, the physician Wegeler, who in collaboration with Ferdinand Ries wrote the *Biographical Notes* which are of such great value. The correspondence between Wegeler and Beethoven was resumed so late as in 1826, when Wegeler was living in Coblenz, and Beethoven mentions that he still has a silhouette portrait of " Lorchen."

The sonata (in C major) is interesting, however, not only because it is the first that Beethoven dedicated to one of the ladies of his choice, but also because it teaches us, with its broken chords, rolling triplets and sextuplets, how memories of the old keyed instrument on which he had practised as a child, the clavi-cymbal (or spinet, as it is more commonly called) ran in his blood. One must not be misled by the fact that Beethoven did not use the term " Hammerklavier " until the very last sonatas. This was due to a late and passing need of getting away from all Italian musical terms whatsoever—a point that will be dealt with later. Meanwhile, in mentioning the piano for which Beethoven wrote his sonatas, a musician should be remembered to whom Beethoven owed much in using this instrument, of comparatively recent date at the time. This was the Italian Muzio Clementi (1752–1832), who was not only an eminent virtuoso on the piano, but also ardently interested in its practical manufacture, its construction and technical development. He was himself a partner in a firm of piano manufacturers in London. As a pianist he was famous, and on his numerous concert tours he was usually accompanied by a troop of pupils— several of whom later became world-renowned performers on the piano. Clementi is at the present day best known as the author of the *Gradus ad Parnassum*. His contemporaries valued his series of piano sonatas, many of which, having regard to the time when they were written, were great in conception and execution, and several of them were found in Beethoven's far from abundant collection of music. Some of Clementi's sonatas, it is true, were modelled on those of Mozart and Beethoven, but even amongst the earlier ones Beethoven would be able to observe a rich and full-toned use of the piano, which meant a decisive step beyond the piano treatment of Philip Emmanuel Bach and Haydn. The long brilliant runs and passages that brighten several movements of the sonatas of his early years, the powerful, rich-toned and bold grasp of chords, the whole of the broad movement that became his enduring characteristic feature, can be traced back to the study of Clementi's sonatas. However dry and reasoned and calculated to display the brilliance of the performer most of them may seem to us at the present day, a few still bear witness to the deeper feeling and inner emotion of their composer.

CHAPTER III

Wɪᴛʜ the next three sonatas, the first that he provided with an opus number, viz. Opus 2, Nos. 1, 2 and 3, we now accompany Beethoven from Bonn to the Austrian capital. Vienna was then, and for many years afterwards, a brilliant city, devoted to art and the pleasures of life. It has often been said that when Beethoven, at the age of twenty-two, migrated thither, it was because he was drawn to it as the home of Mozart and Haydn, and of so many other musicians and virtuosi whose names are now forgotten, but this can hardly have been the only reason. As a matter of fact there was a quite peculiar relation between Bonn and Vienna. The Elector Maximilian was a brother of the Emperor Joseph II of Austria, and the nobility of Vienna and Bonn were closely related by ties of blood and friendship. An exchange between the two cities of young men, for the sake of studies—especially of students from Bonn who were sent to the Austrian capital—was by no means uncommon. Beethoven was therefore not a unique instance. Two of his intimate friends, Wegeler and Breuning, took the same road, the latter, like Beethoven, to stay permanently in Vienna. On the other hand, Count Ferdinand von Waldstein, whom we shall meet later on in the history of the sonatas, took up his residence in Bonn, though he had previously lived in Vienna and afterwards returned to Austria. It was due mainly to his efforts that Beethoven now went to Vienna, with the intention of returning to his native town after a few years of training and study, but destiny—one is perhaps right in saying Beethoven's good destiny—willed otherwise.

In view of this constant intercourse between the aristocratic and artistic circles of Bonn and Vienna, it is not surprising that Beethoven quickly and easily gained admission to the most refined and wealthy houses in which art was cultivated with great interest, and in the *salons* of the nobility, especially, the poor and unknown Bonn musician was a welcome guest. Perhaps this also explains why he had no difficulty in obtaining lessons from Joseph Haydn, who as a rule was very unwilling to receive pupils. The details of Beethoven's studies are outside the scope of these chapters. It is well known that as a teacher Haydn greatly disappointed his young pupil, who consoled himself by seeking guidance from Johannes Schenk,* a musician of much lower standing. Later he studied more systematically under Albrechtsberger and Salieri. Beethoven's choleric temperament once led him so far as to say that Haydn " was not dealing honestly " with him. Suspicion had already taken root in the mind of this young artist.

It was clear to Beethoven, however, that he could learn a great deal from the *works* of Haydn. They were not amongst those which excited the least interest in the circles into which he had gained an entrance. His admiration and reverence for Haydn's genius was unreserved and unalterable, and his dedication of the three sonatas of Opus 2, with which he began his career, was undoubtedly a sincere expression of his feelings, even though he could not go so far as to call himself " a pupil of Haydn " on the title-page. In the dedication the famous old master is called " Docteur en musique," an honorary title conferred upon him by the University of Oxford; it was therefore a reminder of his glorious visits to England. From Beethoven's point of view it would be a matter of courtesy and there is no reason to be of Mr. Shedlock's opinion, that it was an ironical addition.

* Schenk's modest remark to Bauernfeld, that he had only considered himself to be a tool, which had been used in the theoretical training of the future music Titan, deserves to be remembered.

The publishers, in their announcement of the sonatas, say that " they show not only the power possessed by Herr van Beethoven as a pianist, but also the delicacy with which he knows how to handle his instrument." This is an indication that Beethoven was at this time chiefly regarded as a piano virtuoso.

The sonatas were published in 1796, but we can see from a Viennese musical paper that they had been known for some time. Beethoven had played them himself in the *salons*, and hand-written copies, after the manner of the day, no doubt circulated amongst his friends and admirers. Probably Beethoven first played his Opus 2 at the house of Prince Lichnowsky, where his Opus 1 (the trios) was also played for the first time, and where Haydn was also frequently a guest.

In considering the composer of these early sonatas, then, we must keep in mind the pianist who is a distinguished and honoured guest in the *salons* of Viennese society. That is the background of this music, which, in so far as it was composed in Vienna, turns its face to the gay and music-loving world of that city. Taken as a whole, these sonatas do not wear the features of a lonely or introspective man.

From other sources we are acquainted with the Beethoven of these days as a young man who tried, even in his personal appearance, to bring himself on a level with the people whose society he frequented. At that time he was still careful about matters of dress, being almost foppish, with his lorgnette and his coat of fine blue broadcloth with gilt buttons. He learned riding and fencing, nay, even dancing; tradition says, with the sad result that he, the sovereign lord of music, never learned to keep time ! In spite of all this he certainly never gave up one iota of his convictions as an artist, nor of the highly developed spirit of opposition of his strong personality; the history of the sonatas does, in fact, give instances of such conflicts and outbursts of self-assertion. Undoubtedly, too, he must from the

C

very beginning have felt himself above this society and almost have looked down upon it in defiance. Not the least reason for this would be that he soon became aware that the ladies especially were delighted with those " finger acrobats " who were just then carrying everything before them in Vienna and corrupting public taste. He would feel bitterly that these leaders of fashion in Vienna appreciated or understood but rarely what he essentially was, or the ideals to which he was striving to attain. In the minds of most of these people he would be classed on a level with such favourite virtuosi as Wölffl or Gelinek (that wizard of variations), or poor Steibelt of unhappy memory, who obtained great effects with his *tremoli* on the piano, while his beautiful wife accompanied him on the tambourine ! In those circles it was sometimes found interesting—in a sporting musical sense—to back a Beethoven against such fellows as these. It happened only very seldom, however, without some display of his biting humour.*

A favourite form of entertainment in these *salons* consisted of improvisations, which every pianist had to be able to play if he wanted to hold his own with his audiences. But what a gulf there must have been between their runs and trills, their cascades of sound or their musical fireworks, that once made Beethoven wickedly ask one of them : " Yes, but look here, when are you going to begin ? "—and the music that resounded when, on rare occasions, and seldom at an order, he sat down at the piano to improvise, most often when he was in the mood to give his imagination a free rein. Very often, it is true, quite a little comedy had to be acted first to induce him to do so, but when he did yield, the understanding members of his

---

* It is characteristic of the attitude of these other pianists to Beethoven, that so late as in 1818–20, when Czerny had arranged recitals of Beethoven's piano music in his own house every Sunday morning, the limited accommodation was, in the sarcastic words of Schindler, not taken up by any of the virtuosi in such great favour with the general public.

audience spoke of these improvisations with the greatest enthusiasm. It seems as though the most beautiful inspirations of the young Master sprang into life on these occasions ; unfortunately, however, many of them arose and died in the same hour, although Beethoven was always careful with his ideas, and once said that he would be able to repeat an extempore piece of music note by note. The Fantasia for piano, Opus 77, has often been mentioned as a sort of paradigm of the improvisations of Beethoven, but instances of this side of his genius can also be found in the sonatas, as we shall presently see. The powerful impression made by his improvisations has been preserved in a few accounts given by enraptured listeners. We read in them how the Master's figure at the piano seemed to assume a more than earthly aspect ; his eyes blazed and his features were drawn. " It was a grand and yet an awe-inspiring sight." " He knew how to make such an impression that often he drew tears from everyone, and many could be heard weeping."

Our knowledge of Beethoven's piano-playing is, in fact, not a slight one, even though the opinions about it are somewhat varied ; but that is easily explained, partly by the taste and particular artistic style of the narrator in relation to that of Beethoven, partly by the very changeable moods and the impulsive temperament of the latter ; finally, also, it would depend on the period of Beethoven's life in which such a listener had heard him play. It is a well-known fact that as a young man he played the organ, while at the same time he founded his studies of the piano on J. S. Bach's *Wohltemperiertes Clavier*, and Ph. Em. Bach's *Versuch der wahren Art das Clavier zu spielen*. Here then is the firm foundation of his playing and of his technical training, and this especially (the organ and J. S. Bach) explains the importance he attached to legato playing, and which is already illustrated in the broad singing passages in his earliest Vienna sonatas.

Those who had the good fortune to hear Beethoven play were, as said before, most enthusiastic about his free improvisations; but they also speak of the ease with which he played at sight, including music in full score, and transposed on the spot. Nor is he less famed, in his absolute mastery of the piano, for his beauty of tone, its power, its singing quality, its fullness, passion and humour.* It is quite possible, of course, that in the ears of those who had not progressed beyond the ordinary smooth elegance which delighted them in the piano-playing of the drawing-room pianists, Beethoven's autocratic manner might seem "rough" and his method of playing "hard," being in a high degree personal, expressive, sharply emphasised and probably also capricious. Strange to say, even competent musicians like Cherubini and Pleyel, and later Spohr, have expressed such disparaging opinions on Beethoven's playing, probably for reasons like those indicated above. Later generations who have heard a Liszt, a Rubinstein, a Bülow and the greatest of the pianists of the present day, would certainly far better be able to appreciate and admire Beethoven as a piano-player. In this capacity, too, he quickly advanced beyond his time. A few positive statements about his playing, which seem to be reliable and founded on accurate judgment, are of special interest: such as, that Beethoven's attitude while playing was supremely calm, noble and beautiful, and without any grimaces (probably several of his rivals were guilty of something of that kind!); one "never saw any throwing about of the hands, they glided over the keys and the fingers alone did the work." His playing "differed so much from the ordinary style that it seemed as though he would break new ground for himself" (an early remark by a discerning observer). This

---

* "In rapid scales, double trills and skips he was unrivalled. It can be seen from his sketch-books that he attached great importance to finished, flowing, powerful and legato playing. His exercises deal with scales in octaves, thirds, sixths, tenths, double chords, skips, the crossing over and interplay of the hands. Many attempts aim at tone effects, especially the effect of letting a chord die away by lifting the fingers one by one from above" (Huschke).

agrees with Czerny, who wrote in his *School for the Piano*:
"Beethoven enticed new and bold passages from the piano
by the use of the pedal, and by extraordinarily characteristic
playing, which was especially remarkable for the strict *legato*
of the chords and formed a new kind of singing . . . his
playing was spiritual, grandiose, and, particularly in *adagio*,
full of feeling and very romantic. . . . The means of expression
often went to extremes, especially when it was a matter of
humour." It is characteristic of him that he sometimes kept
the tempo back in *crescendo* passages, while as a rule he played
strictly in time and kept exactly to the tempo, yet so that
humour and his varying moods also found expression here,
when he would suddenly hurry the tempo on. Opinions vary
as to his use of the pedal, yet, unlike Mozart, he seems to have
used it much oftener than the indications given in the printed
works. It is said of Beethoven's playing that it was " extremely
brilliant, but not very delicate and sometimes indistinct."
Here again we must take into account his momentary mood,
possibly also his failing sense of hearing. The opinion just
mentioned can hardly be taken as applicable to all occasions,
even though Beethoven would almost certainly sacrifice some
of the delicacy for the sake of greater feeling.* At any
rate it is probably true that Beethoven overcame the greatest
difficulties more by the power of his all-round musical
genius than by the help of perfect technical mastery of the
instrument. As he advanced in his career as a composer he
naturally paid less attention to keeping up his rank as a pianist,
yet he by no means neglected his playing, and as long as his
hearing fairly permitted it, Beethoven continued playing in
public, though more and more rarely. The last time he sat

* This is quite in accord with the remarks of Beethoven's pupil, F. Ries : " When
I spoilt a passage, made a mistake in the attack, or failed in a skip, he seldom said
anything ; but if there was anything wanting in the expression, a crescendo or the
like, or in the character of the piece, he was angry ; because, as he said, the former
might be an accident, the latter a want of knowledge, of feeling or of attention.
The former often happened to himself, even when he was playing in public."

at the piano at a public concert was in 1814, when he took part in his B flat Trio, Opus 97; his deafness was then already very far advanced. For some time he still played in his circle of friends; the accounts of the deaf Master's playing in these later years often sound very fantastic and differ widely. Spohr, who, however, neither understood nor cared about Beethoven, says categorically : " It was certainly no pleasure ! " (to listen to him). A faint afterglow of the character of Beethoven's playing reaches us in accounts of how his best and dearest pupils and admirers played his own compositions. In dealing with the sonata Opus 101 there will be an opportunity to dwell further on this.

    *   *   *   *   *   *

Beethoven had learned to value and look up to the music of Haydn and Mozart and followed them in his first sonatas, which have many of their features both in form and in theme. But at the same time we hear in them at the very outset the voice of a new and independent personality, which increases with astonishing speed in each new opus and develops more and more as it forgets its original source in a greater and greater degree and creates its own form. We already begin to perceive it in the first sonata of Opus 2, in F minor. It begins with a theme that was much in favour at the time, and occurs in the music of Mozart and others : the ascending notes of the broken chord; it has been called, from its origin and effect, " The Mannheim rocket." (The beginning of the second sonata seems to point in the same direction.) The *andante* is an arrangement of a piano quartet from the Bonn days, one of the youthful first attempts on a bigger scale. Even at this early stage we notice Beethoven's well-known inclination to return to his themes and clothe them in a more beautiful and significant form. This movement, regarded as a whole, is closely akin to the art of Mozart, but for *our* ears it is impossible to detect such misery and utter despair as the young composer ascribed to it in the naïve and hurried text of a subjoined ode, notwithstanding its melancholy tone.   The minuet that follows it, according to Haydn's pattern, is not so childlike or spontaneous as the corresponding movements of its predecessor. It is already more emphasised and more gloomy in theme (although Haydn also wrote a few peculiar minuets in a minor key), and it has almost given up that air of dance music in which this part of the sonata originated.   It already points onward to the Beethoven *scherzi*, soon in a singular way to obtain their place in the sonatas.   But—in the *finale* especially —a new and particularly Beethovenesque feature appears. With regard to this movement it is worth while noticing that the F minor sonata was written, or at any rate sketched out, in Bonn.   This *finale* has nothing to do with society life in Vienna.   It is passionate, sombre, violent, like the youth in the sad home in the town on the Rhine.   There seems to be a strong, personal outburst in the first, brusquely struck chords, and in the contrasting, mournfully plaintive melodies, the spontaneous singing of a youthful soul ; one of them is that beautiful second theme, that like a timid sigh comes out shyly to a gentler world than that described in the harsh minor chords and passages, and which, after being twice repeated, is concluded with apparent reluctance as though by a stern command.   This early sonata, then, bears the stamp of the Beethoven features, and the *finale* especially, with its dramatic passion, makes one feel that it has been conceived in a new era : that of Werther's *Leiden*, of the Great Revolution, the era of the hectic dramas of Schiller's youth.   In the sonatas of Haydn and Mozart, the closing movement was nearly always—no matter how agitated and varying its different stages—harmonious, well-balanced, frequently comfortable, nay even " jolly " and therefore often its least weighty part.   What a contrast to them is this first great sonata of Beethoven !   Here— as in most of the succeeding ones—he has already gathered and saved up his force for this very final movement, in order to make it the weighty, irresistibly effective close of the work, the conscious climax of the sonata.

The next two sonatas of Opus 2 were now composed in Vienna, and this can be distinctly perceived in them. *They* do not gruffly, not to say harshly, turn their backs on the surrounding world. Their brilliant attitude, so favourable to the display of the performer's talent, shows exactly the composer's intention of distinguishing himself as much as possible in the circle of his Viennese patrons, who expected him, as they expected every new virtuoso who appeared on the scene, to produce compositions of his *own*. In these sonatas, or at any rate in the greater part of them, one seems to read some of the joy and pride of their creator in seeing such a radiant world, full of promise, opening to receive the first fruits of his genius.

There is an assured gaiety and courage in them; they are elaborated with a greater richness, brilliance and variety, both in harmonics and subject, as well as in a pianistic aspect, than the first, which is altogether remote from them in its introspective and personal intensity.

The A major sonata shows the bright joy and pride of the composer in his own achievement, in the very conquest of difficulties, both musical and technically instrumental. Haydn's gaiety is heard in the first movement, and his spirit is present in the splendid and inventive thematic work—though developed and multiplied. The F minor sonata, especially the *finale*, contains nothing of this, which is another proof of its pre-Vienna origin. In the modulation part we meet with a Beethoven idea, also occurring later in the sonatas and elsewhere, that of letting the leading theme appear in its full form but in an alien key (here F major instead of A), as if the composer wanted to "trick" the listener into thinking that he has "got home" again, while he still has a few surprises up his sleeve, before he correctly and normally returns to the tonic key. This peculiarity of style has been called "Pseudo-reprise," and justly been referred back to Haydn's mode of expression, but its humorous character, that seems to lay a playful trap for the listener, is closely related to Beethoven's artistic nature, and it occurs frequently, especially in the sonatas of his earlier years, such as in Opus 10, No. 2 (1st movement), Opus 14, No. 2 (1st movement). The melody, hinted at rather than distinctly sung, of the second theme is a characteristic feature in this *allegro ;* we shall see that Beethoven is often fond of expressing himself in this way. The *Largo*, which is called *appassionato*, is related to pathetic and exalted slow movements in Haydn, while lacking the sweetness of Mozart. It will be noticed that Beethoven here already introduces an "orchestral" feature in his piano music : the *pizzicato* effect of the basses, doubtless an invention of his own. He is entirely himself, too, in his surprising *minor* transformation of the leading theme advancing boldly and broadly in full force. There is good reason for Combarieu to say of this *Largo* as a whole, that "already it is the work of a thinker." The third movement is called a *Scherzo*, for the first time in the series of the sonatas. In idea and subject, however, it is mostly akin to Haydn's playfulness, and, as sometimes in this, it contains a colour-note of Slav sadness in the minor theme of the trio. The object of the Rondo seems mainly to be that of social entertainment.

In the third of the sonatas (C major), which makes still greater demands on the performer, one is reminded rather of Mozart. The first movement is an elaboration of a quartet movement from the Bonn period. An insight into this peculiar method is easily obtained in Riemann's *Handbuch der Musikgeschichte*,[1] showing the energetic, untiring alterations and improvements, in which inspiration and intention form a deep, strange and often extraordinarily fruitful alliance. It will be observed that the little theme with which the movement now

[1] Vol. II. Part III. p. 196 seq.

begins, and which may seem to be insignificant, somewhat arid, if you like, is a clever re-modelling of the opening theme of the quartet, which was a more conventional and empty musical phrase, compared to which the C major theme in its present form has a quite bold and distinct air.   In this movement a joy, brimming over, like that so often occurring in Mozart, is developed with this theme ; it is full of radiant youthful courage, that at times surges up to proud defiance, and of the humour that is and always will be an unfading feature of Beethoven's musical physiognomy.   This humour cannot be sufficiently emphasised in view of the prevalent talk of his morbid melan- choly and super-sensuous ideality.   In his life as in his art Beethoven kept this humour of his, preserving it safely through the saddest trials, even up to the closing days of his life.   We meet continual instances of it in the sonatas.   This sonata has two examples ; one in the second movement which is the first real *Scherzo* (with Coda) in the series of sonatas, and the character of which is easily distinguishable from the Haydn– Mozartian minuet movement—the find of a young master !— and the other in the *finale*.   Both have the impress of that almost giddy feeling of victory over the burden of life, which is a typical trait in the spiritual physiognomy of this " Storm and Stress " period.   It leaps out to us here in the onward-rushing passages of sixths, and laughs at us ; it is giddy too, though in another way, in that second theme, that reminds one of the *finale* of the so-called " Champagne trio," Opus 1, G major, which is about contemporaneous with it. The movement is one entire joy of life, gaiety, triumph.   But next to Mozart's happy spirit the sonata is an evidence of what the virtuoso style of Clementi meant for the young Beethoven. In the rolling octave passages in the first movement, the strangely free Coda with the surprising A flat episode and great Cadenza, as well as the chain of trills in the *finale*, one is reminded of the concertos.   Just at this time Beethoven did actually enter upon this field with the B flat major and C major Concertos. Set against all the radiant brilliance and *bravura* of the other movements of the sonata is its *adagio* in E major. Here the young Master has retired into himself; he has felt the need of self-communing and now writes a dreamy music-poem, passionate and exalted; it is the forerunner of other introspective and deeply emotional movements in later sonatas and other works. The *minor* section with the sharply marked bars is peculiar with its crossing of the hands and syncopated notes emphasised by accents. This part is altogether particularly Beethoven in character—and psychologically extremely interesting. The young Master rises to great pathos later in this beautiful passage, in which C major appears suddenly, through a very effective deceptive cadence.

CHAPTER IV

THE three sonatas of Opus 2 are followed in the very next year, 1797, by a new piano sonata, Opus 7 in E flat major. It was called in the publishers' announcements " Grande Sonate," a term here used for the first time, and it is dedicated, with a dainty French title, to Mademoiselle la Comtesse Babette de Keglevics. We are still in the circle of Beethoven's aristocratic acquaintances, but can hardly suppose that the dedication of the sonata to a young lady of rank was due to tender feelings on the part of the composer. At one time it certainly was called " Die Verliebte," but that was probably because the Countess Babette was considered to be one of Beethoven's numerous so-called " flames," who were well known in these circles, and perhaps Viennese society judged from a dedication really founded on Beethoven's feelings. The music itself of the sonata cannot exactly be described as " enamoured "; besides, there is no evidence that the Countess was one of those who had stirred Beethoven's affections. He may have paid her some attention—this would not have been unusual with him, and as the lady's music-master he would have ample opportunity—but in any case he would wish to pay her and her aristocratic family a customary compliment by dedicating his new piano work to her. Possibly he had played it for the first time in her home, which was situated just opposite the house in which he was then living. A year or two later the Countess was married and became Princess Odescalchi, but the friendly relations between the two continued, and Beethoven dedicated to the Princess his Concerto in C, which, although composed earlier, was not printed until 1801. It has been said by a

relative of the young Countess that Beethoven used to come
to the lessons " in dressing-gown and slippers, and with a
nightcap on his head." It does not sound very probable, and
in any case it disagrees with the accounts we have of Beethoven
just at this time, trying to adapt himself in appearance to the
society in which he moved.

Compared with the three first sonatas the character of this
one is calmer and more harmonious. It does not give that
impression of wanting to attract attention and create a sensation, as do the first sonatas, at àny rate the two in major keys.
Beethoven had by this time settled down to his life in Vienna,
which he had very quickly decided that he would not re-
exchange for that in Bonn. He had already made himself at
home in his new world and knew how to value its reception
of him. He had been away on the only concert tour he was
ever to undertake, to Prague and to Berlin, where he played
at Court, and probably this strengthened his self-confidence.
He was able to forget, at times, or to rise above, the envy with
which the musicians of Vienna received him, because they saw
in him a redoubtable rival, and gave vent to their envy in the
correspondence of a Leipzig musical paper. It was during this
year that he wrote home, to Dr. Wegeler : " I am getting on
well ; I may say, continually better and better," a statement
that was unusually sober-minded and contented for him.

It is this state of mind that finds a voice in the broadly
planned and joyously gliding first movement, the second subject
of which contains a lingering, yearning beauty. The closing
theme of the first part is singularly fanciful, with its great
pedal-point and the melodious figuration in which it seems to
be veiled. The modulation part seems strangely short in a
movement otherwise rather comprehensive, until it becomes
clear that here, more than in Opus 2, No. 3, space has been
kept for the broadly planned, typically Beethovenesque Coda,
which partly takes the place of, or rather supplements, the

modulation part. Thus it develops the second subject which has not been used in the modulatory part itself. The sonata reaches its highest point, however, in the *Largo*. Altogether, in these early sonatas, the most personal features are frequently to be found in the slow movements ; it is as though the young Master resorted to them for that introspection for which there was less opportunity in the rapid and brilliant outer movements that were more turned towards the outer world. This *Largo* is prominent among the early ones because of its tenderness and broad pathos (in the A flat and D flat melodies respectively), and for the first time in Beethoven's piano music we get a vivid impression of what the pauses mean in it ; of how he speaks to us also in the pause, nay, not least in the pause, how it, too, seems to sing its part in its momentous silence. Certainly Haydn and Mozart knew how to use the pause with masterly effect ; the former especially, in a humorous way. In this instance Beethoven's use of it, as so often later in instrumental works, is one of great seriousness. The powerful, dynamic effects, too, are very noticeable in this *Largo*, they remind one of Beethoven's growing interest in orchestral work and give the music a peculiar, accented style, now pathetic, now whimsical ; nay, one actually feels here how Beethoven has enjoyed pushing his effects to extremes, and surprising and disconcerting his listeners, an inheritance from Joseph Haydn and the Mannheim school of which he made good use. When playing such a movement, therefore, one cannot pay too much attention to the expression marks. Beethoven bestowed minute care on their accuracy, and the effect of the performance depends entirely on carrying out exactly the composer's directions in this respect.

The sonata has neither a *scherzo* nor a *minuet*. Its third movement is simply termed an *allegro*. It is a remarkable piece, and if it had been found in a Schumann composition it would have been called " Intermezzo " or the like. The suggestion of Schumann's name in connection with it is not fortuitous. The comfortable cheerfulness of the allegro, and still more its very fantastic, furtively rustling *minore* (E flat minor), are like forerunners of the later composers for piano of the romantic school. Without any model before him Beethoven here points ahead far beyond his own time. The obscure, mysteriously changing harmonies, the veiled melody, hinted at rather than expressed, have a strangely impressionistic character which has only in later times been adopted and used. The *minore* is one of those *scherzi*, of which there are not a few, which are more remarkable and weighty than the chief movement itself. How Franz Schubert must have enjoyed playing such a movement! The *finale* is that part of the sonata in which one might perhaps be justified in discovering the tender feelings for the young lady whose name Beethoven had placed at the head of his work. It is a very charming, amiable and sprightly piece of music—assuredly not any confession of love, but, if you like, perhaps a not improbable and light love-*making* to the very young Viennese Countess; the most " enamoured " passage will then be found towards the end, in the surprising, extremely charming turn to E major (*pp*) and the subsequent return to the leading key.

*   *   *   *   *   *

The next sonatas again—as in Opus 2—appear as a triad, united under the number of one work : Opus 10, Nos. 1, 2 and 3. They were published only a year after Opus 7. This quite agrees with the foregoing account of Beethoven and his position with regard to Viennese society, that during this period he devoted himself particularly to the composition of music for piano which he could bring with him and perform for the first time in these circles, and which his friends and pupils would be glad to purchase when it was obtainable in print. The sonatas are again dedicated to a lady of the Vienna aristocracy : the Countess Browne. It is significant enough that before their publication a young music-dealer, Joseph Eder, who published them, and who did not belong to one of the old-established firms with whom Beethoven was already connected, opened a subscription in order to get his expenses covered, " as the name of the author (des Herrn Verfassers) is a sufficient guarantee for the quality of his work." The publisher doubtless reckoned on obtaining subscribers from the aristocratic circles.

In dedicating his works to these members of the aristocracy, as was his usual custom, Beethoven intended to pay them his voluntary homage and at the same time to show his appreciation of their kindness and their generous admission of him into their circle. Such dedications had previously in most cases been a refined form of begging. The composer knew, at any rate, that his dedication would as a rule be acknowledged by a sum of money, a costly " snuff-box " or the like. It went against Beethoven's proud and self-reliant spirit to follow this custom. In this, too, he is the first of a new age, in demanding as an artist to be placed on an equal footing with the aristocrats whom he met ; even more, to be ranked above them. There is evidence of this in a great number of oral and written statements, often made in his most drastic manner. Yet, on the other hand, he would find it perfectly right and fitting that these wealthy magnates should admit him to their homes, secure him a life free from care, and satisfy his modest requirements with regard to everything that could make life beautiful and pleasant. He therefore accepted as a matter of course an invitation to take up his quarters for a long time in Prince Lichnowsky's home (we hear more, later, of this patron of Beethoven), but it certainly did not restrict his freedom in any respect, especially not that of his tongue. Once, when he calls Count Browne, to whose wife the sonatas of Opus 10 were dedicated, " the first Mæcenas of my muse," it is most likely because he meant in this way to annoy Prince Lichnowsky, with

whom his relations were just then strained, Lichnowsky really
having the best claim to be called Beethoven's first protector
in Vienna.   In any case he considered Count Browne his special
benefactor, and the latter did, in fact, exert himself a great
deal on behalf of the young composer.   As a token of thanks
for the dedication to the Countess he presented Beethoven with
a magnificent horse.   Beethoven, however, had given up
showing his prowess as a horseman ; he rode only very seldom
and at last quite forgot his valuable mount, so that the groom
was able undisturbed to make a good income in hiring out the
animal, until a big bill for fodder for his " sonata-horse "
reminded Beethoven of its existence, on which he promptly
sold it !   The Count's wife was of Livonian origin, a gifted
pianist and very beautiful.   There was every reason, then, for
Beethoven, who did not willingly avoid beautiful women, to
dedicate his sonata to her !

As for the Count, he was a gay and pleasure-loving Viennese
of Irish descent; he " revelled in pleasures," and Beethoven's
pupil, Ferdinand Ries, annoyed his strict master by joining
in them rather too often.   One cannot imagine that the
Count's appreciation of Beethoven would be very deep ;
nevertheless we hear later that the sonata Opus 22 is dedicated
to him, while two works with variations have been crowned by
Beethoven with the name of the pianist countess, which is also
connected with the undedicated sonata, Opus 31, of which
more will be said later.   A few years after, they both disappeared from Beethoven's sphere of life ; possibly the Count
left Vienna in order to go as Ambassador to St. Petersburg.

*   *   *   *   *   *

The triad of sonatas reaches its climax in the third. We must
be brief in dealing with the two that precede it.   The first, in
C minor, has not inaptly been compared to the famous Mozart
sonata in the same key.   There is a Mozartian vivacity and buoyancy in the spirited main theme, great energy in the powerfully

D

effective leaps to the mediant beyond the octave, and in the bearing of this movement there is a singular clearness and purity which is almost academic. One does not feel as yet what the C minor key was to mean to Beethoven. In the *andante* there is a melodious sweetness that is again reminiscent of Mozart; but in the *finale*, with its frequent *f*'s and *ff*'s, the forceful individuality of a Beethoven again comes into play, and one of his favourite and typical rhythmic motives, | ♩ ♪♪♪ | ♩ |, incidentally occurs in it. The whole movement is extremely concise, nothing in it is superfluous, everything is expressed with perfect clearness and precision. This *finale*, and the sonata as a whole, makes an impression on our generation of a very simple, clear and easily understood " classical " piece of music. It is strange to learn that contemporary listeners had quite another opinion about it, for it can hardly have been mere professional envy that caused the critic in the above-mentioned *Allgemeine Musikalische Zeitung* to describe the sonata as " a piece of music in which the abundance of ideas made the composer pile up his thoughts one upon the other, and in a somewhat bizarre manner group them together in such a way that not rarely they produced an obscure subtlety or a subtle obscurity." Which shows how appreciation and judgment change with the changing times ! And what an insight these few lines of " professional " criticism give us into what Beethoven had to fight against as a creative artist from the very beginning of his career ! There is no *minuet* (nor *scherzo*) in this sonata; this is of some interest, Beethoven having planned an intermediate piece which he calls " Intermezzo " in the sketch-book, adding the remark, " Durchaus so ohne Trio, nur ein Stück." Such an intermezzo—but *with* a trio—occurs in the following F major sonata.

Perhaps some traits of Beethoven's other great model, Haydn, will be found in this Sonata in F, at any rate in the brimming gaiety that goes through the whole of the first movement, rising in the *finale* to frolicsome, even exuberant, spirits in masterly *fugato* play. But it cannot be denied that we encounter here a bolder jesting, a broader humour than that of Haydn, which is jolly and rather homely, and a whimsical, almost mocking smile where Beethoven (in the second part of the first movement) makes use of the so-called " Pseudo-reprise," mentioned above as occurring in the Sonata in A major, Opus 2, No. 2. Here it appears very distinctly, the leading theme (in the modulation part) coming forward first in a " wrong " key, as though with the set purpose of making the listeners forget what the right one was—after which the composer in a couple of bars seems to turn a graceful somersault in order to fall elegantly on his feet in the right key of F major—a genuine display of Beethovenesque humour, which occurs as it were more consciously and deliberately than in his more simple predecessor. The *finale* has been aptly described by Marx as a frolicsome fooling with sonata and fugue : the sonata form is not strictly carried out, and there is really no suggestion of a fugue ; but the composer, being in a mood for playful banter, pretends that a *learned* piece of music of this sort is looming up.

In the gaiety of this *finale* one must be careful not to hurry the piece into an unreasonable rapidity, and thus in reality weaken its effect. It is true that this 2/4 movement is headed " Presto," and the speed that *can* preserve mastery and distinctness in its performance is, of course, allowable. But the *tempi* were not so rapid in Beethoven's time as in these days of express trains and electric currents ; and Mozart was quite right when he did not want his music to be " chased " by a too headlong *tempo*—on the excellent grounds that " the fire from a piece of music must come from within, you will not put more fire into it by hounding it on." This gay sonata, however, has an *allegretto*, neither a *scherzo* nor a *minuet*, but (as in Opus 7 and as planned in the C minor sonata) an intermezzo-like movement. This gloomy, passionate F minor piece with its trio in D flat, in the dreamy beauty of which one involuntarily remembers the name of Franz Schubert, takes us far from the spiritual sphere of Haydn and from the merriment of the outer movements. One sees their playful humour and childish pranks in a new light when one reads Beethoven's letters of this period, especially those to Baron von Zmeskall, his "Music-Count" ("Conte di musica"), who during these years had become one of Beethoven's friends, and on whose worthy and helpful head the young Master never tired of pouring the vials of his radiant spirits, or his always ingenious and really good-natured mockery. Here again we see the harmony between Beethoven's humanity and his artistic production.

The third sonata of this Opus—in D major—should be rather more carefully considered. It is, although Beethoven himself does not call it so, a " Grande Sonate "—which really means a work on concert scale both in compass, plan and development.* It is, moreover, a sonata containing a slow movement, which more than any of the earlier ones vividly expresses Beethoven's personality and his spiritual state at the time when the idea for it was conceived, giving to his despondency the most distinct and earnest features, and long remaining unsurpassed in musical and psychological interest in the series of the sonatas.

The first movement is full of virile power, of dashing courage, and the lovely, slightly melancholy second theme—which may be a reminiscence of a Clementi sonata—is neither capable of, nor intended to dim, the brightness of the movement. The artistic effect of contrast to the *Largo* was to be all the greater, the more this first part radiated power and vital courage, nay,

* Riemann has incidentally maintained that the term " Grande Sonate " was applied to sonatas that were published singly, *i.e.* not in sheets containing two or three or more together, as was often the case in those days. However, as a sonata like that in F minor, Opus 57, which was published singly, is not called " Grande Sonate," the explanation does not meet the case, and Riemann admits this himself. There is more reason to think that the compass and character of a sonata would as a rule be deciding factors in the choice of this term.

almost defiance, and in this respect the Coda is worth noticing, with its *fortissimo* ending, that seems to have been gained by the exertion of force.

The entirely different mood of the *Largo* is therefore all the more impressive. We feel at once that this glorious movement holds a deep melancholy, an ominous pondering, a despondent brooding over an aching pain, which the artist cannot throw off in spite of distinct efforts to free himself. The indisputable, spiritual meaning of the music might be due to an accidental mood, or embody an idea of the artist's imagination, or be ascribed to certain exterior events or experiences that had filled him with a grief for which he sought consolation in the poetry of sounds. The *Largo* has been ascribed to Beethoven's well-known fondness for Shakespeare and considered to be a description of Romeo at the grave of Juliet. But is it possible to believe this ? Does it satisfy either mind or imagination to explain this deeply personal music as a kind of illustration, as reproducing in musical notes a tragic scene from the work of another genius ? There might be more reason to agree with those who have called the movement " At my mother's grave." We know how attached Beethoven was to his mother—particularly in comparison with his feelings for his father—and how deeply he was affected when he was called away from his first stay in Vienna to her sick-bed and her death soon after. The home of his childhood was really broken up when his mother died, and with his affectionate heart he would undoubtedly often dwell on her memory. The theme of the *Largo,* therefore, *may* have arisen in his mind in such an hour, but we have nothing definite to support this view ; and the fact must not be overlooked that more than ten years had elapsed since these events took place. His grief could no longer be so fresh nor his mind so crushed by pain and despair. It is far more reasonable to suppose that at the time when the *Largo* was written, Beethoven was beginning to feel seriously

that his hearing was growing weaker. During these years he
had the first warnings of the terrible fate that was to overtake
him, his deafness. He brooded over this fate, tried to hide it
from others, perhaps he also thought he could deceive himself
and that it was not serious and inevitable. But his fate was
upon him—he could hardly doubt about that ; and even though
he might forget it in the gay life of Vienna and enjoy the favour
shown him, or comfort himself with the consciousness of his
mental and physical powers, he could not wholly escape from
the burden, nor for very long at a time. This burden of sorrow
must already then have swept over his spirit. This *Largo e
mesto*, therefore, became one of those works which are born of
the pain and suffering of an artist for our joy and edification,
as Heine has said, " Aus meinen grossen Schmerzen mach' ich
die kleinen Lieder." It is less easy to explain the connection
between this deeply felt and impressive *Largo* and the movements that follow it, the pleasant but not very considerable
Menuetto and the closing *Rondo*, which seems to be amiably
questioning or searching. Can it be explained as a fulfilment
of the psychological law by which human nature can bear only
a certain measure of sorrow and anguish ? When the measure
is full, a reaction sets in, bringing forgetfulness or repose in
gentler moods, in remembering happier times, to a mind not
morbidly weakened. Beethoven's own interpretation of the
first theme as a sympathising " Are you still so grieved ? "
would seem to indicate this.

Beethoven himself is said to have called the *Largo* a description of the varying moods of a melancholy mind, nor is there
any doubt about the prevailing mood of this movement. It
is produced, musically, by the very choice of key, the irre-
concilable, gloomy D minor—Berlioz has even called it " bleak "
—by the low notes of the melody, which remind one of
the sombre colouring of a contralto voice, and by its almost
obstinate, or, if you like, hopeless, despairing circling about

the same few notes. The violently dissonant outbursts in full chords have all the character of despair. This hopeless brooding is most powerfully and impressively described towards the close, in which the melody is laid in the deepest bass, where it is woven into a web of disquieting and ominous broken chords, and raised through apparently remote keys (a bold musical effect, which is really logical enough) to a wilder and wilder expression. Reconciliation does not come, not even at the end ; it is more like the plaintive sigh of exhaustion than repose.

It cannot be wondered that Beethoven was deeply and violently shaken when he discovered that his hearing was attacked, and growing weaker in spite of all the remedies attempted. He was being plundered and ravaged on a vital point ; he was in danger of losing the most important, the greatest of all the senses. To him it must have looked like the complete and undreamed-of overthrow of his career as an artist, fatal to him as an executant musician and destructive of his whole position and future in the musical world of Vienna. He did, in fact, feel the misfortune to be a fate in the antique sense, as an evil from which he could not escape and which had been laid upon him by the gods (or, as he calls them in the famous *Testament of Heiligenstadt*, the Parcæ), whom he had to fight against and " seize by the throat." Was the fate laid upon him, and was it so laid without any fault of his own ? Two questions will perhaps never be answered : whether the thought suggested itself to Beethoven that he was himself to blame for this suffering, and what grounds can be discovered for this thought in the actual facts. Once the question was raised, and it seems to have been raised for the first time in Grove's famous *Dictionary of Music*, it could not fail to make a deep impression on everyone, because such a self-caused suffering might explain much that was otherwise obscure in Beethoven's inner life and in his conduct. A doubly tragic background would then be given to this *Largo*, the first violent outbreak of his deep melancholy. But notwithstanding the research and thorough examination of this case by medical scientists, it seems no longer possible to arrive at a clear and definite result. It will probably always remain an unsolved problem.*

Beethoven mentions his deafness for the first time in a letter of June 29, 1800 (?), to Dr. Wegeler, and expresses himself with such openness and keen observation that physicians at this very day have thought they could diagnose his complaint (otosclerosis); it is probably only as to its cause and origin that doubt and disagreement still exist. He writes in a letter of " that malicious demon : my poor health," and he states with reason that it is caused by an internal ailment. He talks of various cures that he has been made to go through in vain (and which, by the way, he was to continue for a long while, now in desperation, now in hopefulness). He particularly mentions that he can no longer hear the high notes (in vocal and instrumental music); it causes him less discomfort in conversation, as people do not notice his dull hearing very much, knowing that he is absent-minded ; but he has " a roaring and swishing noise in his ears night and day " (the typical and distressing feature of ear-trouble). He cannot force himself to tell people that he is deaf and he adjures his friend not to tell anyone of his state, " not even Lorchen " (*i.e.* Eleonore Breuning). " I only tell you about it as a secret. I have already often cursed my existence ; Plutarch has led me to resignation " —but soon after he calls resignation " a miserable refuge, and yet there is nothing else left for me."

Such deep despondency would of necessity find utterance in

* The latest writer on Beethoven's infirmity (W. Schweisheimer : *Beethoven's Leiden*, Munich, 1922) rejects the diagnosis of Otosclerosis, and is of the opinion that Beethoven suffered from a disease of the inner ear, Neuritis acustica. Neither this complaint, nor the disease which according to this writer caused Beethoven's death, a Cirrhosis of the liver, can, as explained by him, be ascribed to self-incurred infection, when no direct " evidence " of this is given. Such evidence has not been given and in the nature of the case it probably never will. Meanwhile this book contains a great deal that is valuable and interesting with regard to the influence of Beethoven's deafness on his production, the history of his disease, etc.

his music, and at this time it was nowhere so strongly uttered as in the *Largo* in D minor.*   Yet in reality Beethoven had not resigned himself to his fate, nor was he yet quite hopeless.   He could still enjoy the society of other people ; he took part in various ways in the musical life about him—perhaps he also expected to be able to preserve enough of the failing faculty to keep him ,from being excluded from society.   The consciousness that he was hard of hearing was now almost a benefit to the exaggerated anxiety with regard to his health that had long held sway over his mind.   (At the age of twenty-five, when he thought himself consumptive, he had already written the well-known words, " In spite of the weakness of my body my soul shall rule.")   His deafness developed but slowly for a time, and, as so often happens in cases of chronic complaints, Beethoven was able, periodically, to forget to a certain extent, or even to reconcile himself to, his infirmity, his unusually strong character and firm will, of course, coming greatly to his aid.   We can understand his optimism then, his inflexible courage and the bright gaiety that still for a long time characterises him and speaks to us in his music—including that of the piano sonatas.   Whether this explains the changes or contrasts of mood mentioned above, between the *Largo* and *Minuet*, and the *Finale*, is perhaps a question.   Perhaps the deeper-lying cause is that Beethoven had not yet reached that interior maturity and that mastery over his art that was to enable him later to carry out fully the principle of his compositions in sonata form : the fusion of the individual parts within the cycle into a unity.

---

* With regard to the performance of the *Largo*, Czerny has this statement : " In this *Largo* a carefully calculated *Ritardando* and *Accelerando* must enhance the effect." Schindler writes of it : " According to Beethoven the performance of this comprehensive movement requires that the *tempo* should be varied about ten times—which is, however, perceptible mostly to a delicate ear.   The leading theme, on its return, keeps its first *tempo*, while all the others undergo a change, and must be mutually balanced according to the requirements of musical perception."   These statements by men who had heard the Master's own recital of the *Largo* give one a slight idea of his *rubato* performance, in the best sense of the term, of this piece.

CHAPTER V

BEETHOVEN himself calls the following sonata, Opus 13 in C minor, " Pathétique," whereas titles like the " Moonlight," the " Pastoral Sonata " and the " Appassionata " have been invented by romantic admirers or by publishers with an eye for advertisement. That he gave it this title himself makes one feel tempted to connect it with the gravity of the affliction dealt with in the previous chapter, and understand its real meaning to be one full of suffering, the sonata being written at a time when Beethoven had become fully aware of the seriousness of his malady. Yet there is more reason to think that the term " pathétique " should be understood in an æsthetic sense, as the expression of exalted passion, and then the reason for choosing it is not far to seek. Enthusiasm for the ideals of antiquity was prevalent at the time and found expression in other contemporary art. There can be no doubt that for a time Beethoven also came under its influence, more, perhaps, than has often been noticed. It is well known that during this period Vienna eagerly followed the example of Paris in taking ancient Rome as a model, even in the fashion of clothes and of hair-dressing. Beethoven himself at this time had his unruly hair cut " Titus fashion," as a certain mode of wearing the hair was called. But beyond these external details, which may have been a passing fancy, there is evidence that he was more deeply influenced by this antique movement. We have heard him mention Plutarch as his example in resignation, and speak not of " Fate " but of the Parcæ; he is absorbed in Plato, and one Beethoven scholar (Kalischer) has pointed out that a quotation in one of Beethoven's letters indicates a knowledge of Anaxagoras, a Greek philosopher unknown to the average man. Beethoven mentions Pericles as an example to be followed; and we are all acquainted with his enthusiasm for the republican, the classic Roman form of government, and its highest European representative, the young Napoleon Bonaparte. His homage to this genius soon after, in the " Eroica " Symphony, is unmistakably anti-heroic in character.

This strictly classical tendency seems already noticeable in the lesser C minor sonata (Opus 10, No. 1), not without reason sometimes called the " Little Pathétique." In Opus 13 the plan is broader, the style greater, the attitude more conscious, and it is noticeable that the same key has been chosen in both cases. The pathos that we now meet with in the " Pathétique Sonata " is, as it were, akin to the characters of classic tragedy, and, it may be added, as they appeared in their French renaissance; Beethoven's choice of a French title in this unique instance is perhaps, therefore, not accidental. This sonata music is beautiful, exalted and full of earnestness, power and pomp, but we are not so tenderly affected by it, nor so close to the artist's heart as in the *Largo* in Opus 10, No. 3. His manner seems rather to be cool, dignified certainly, and with a look of pain about the drawn lips, but at the same time he is, as it were, self-conscious in his pain and watchful in regard to giving it the right effective expression. In the really pathetic introductory *Grave* we are at once aware of the dignified, self-conscious throw of the toga with which the figures of the tragedy step forth upon the stage, their classical bearing while they impart to us the story of their fate and their sufferings. This *Grave*, which is sounded three times in the course of the sonata, and which is reflected at the beginning of the second part of the *Allegro*, is the core of the movement, which receives its character from it. The *Allegro* is certainly more full of feeling, but, like the *Grave*, it is controlled by a certain classic, reserved outline and shows no particular desire to take the listeners into its confidence. One of Beethoven's favourite effects as a pianist is introduced into the second subject, that of crossing the hands—perhaps also an indication with regard to the character and intention of the movement. In the *Adagio Cantabile* we seem to get nearer to the composer's heart. It is a melodious and noble piece with delicate and beautiful details and adorned with bold, harmonic transitions, but it is not really pathetic music, and its plastic beauty seems to have been the composer's chief concern, witness the " decorous " classicism of the close. A *Scherzo* would hardly suit the whole character of the sonata; Beethoven therefore omits this intermediate part, as in the " Little Pathétique." The attack in the *Finale* is pathetic perhaps, but in another way than that of the first movement. It is as though the gentle singing of the *Adagio* had introduced a softer mood. This *Finale* has even been called " tändelnd "—a term which there can only be reason to apply to the inconsiderable second subject. The connection with the first movement, however, can be distinctly read in the leading subject of the *Finale*, its relationship to the second one hardly being accidental, and perhaps being an indication of the aim, lately referred to, at unity in a sonata work. Beethoven with a firm hand keeps hold of the ominous C minor in his *Finale*, and he does not bring about any close in a major key. The effectively calculated and strong closing accents put the finishing mark of the " pathetic " on this work, which was long in extraordinary favour, and perhaps may be called the most " classic " of all the sonatas, a work of art typical of Beethoven at this time.

The original title of the sonata was " *Grande Sonate Pathétique*," therefore an immediate indication of concert style. It was published towards the end of 1799 and was dedicated to Prince Carl Lichnowsky, who, as we have heard, was one of those who at the beginning exerted themselves on behalf of the young Bonn musician when he came to Vienna, perhaps at the recommendation of Count von Waldstein. The Prince—who belonged to a Polish family—was twelve years older than Beethoven, an ardent amateur of music and a talented pianist. He was a pupil of Mozart, for whom, at a critical moment in that composer's life, he obtained admission to the Court at Berlin and the possibility of a permanent appointment there. Mozart, however, out of affection for " his Emperor," could not make up his mind to accept it. Prince Lichnowsky and his wife, *née* Countess Thun, a beautiful and musically gifted woman, now interested themselves in him who was " to console them for the loss of Mozart," so much that they even placed a couple of rooms in their mansion at his disposal. During the years 1794–6, when Beethoven was not staying in the country near Vienna, he was thus the guest of this prince, to whom he had already dedicated his Opus 1 (the three Trios, 1795). It would probably be in this house that he was first introduced into the society of the Austrian aristocracy, amongst whom he found enduring friends and benefactors. It can hardly have been the prefix " van " to his name that gained him admission to these circles, in which it was felt to be but a duty becoming to rank to encourage and support a young musical genius and an eminent pianist, and to bear with Beethoven's not infrequent caprices, or even lack of ordinary good manners. This might, of course, result in friction and unpleasant incidents, from which even the relations with Prince Lichnowsky were not always free. Although the Prince himself had shown the young composer such a distinguishing mark of his respect as ordering his servants to attend to Beethoven before attending to himself, situations arose in which the sensitive, self-assertive and hot-tempered musician took offence or felt himself treated with contumely. It was during such a period of hostility that Beethoven, as stated above, in a spirit of defiance proclaimed Count Browne as his " first Mæcenas," but the breach was

healed again, and Beethoven soon after honoured his true
Mæcenas with the dedication of his second, D major symphony.
A more serious rupture occurred in 1806, while the Prince was
residing at his country house in Silesia where the composer
was his guest, but in that case one's sympathy is entirely with
Beethoven. This episode is of some interest in the history
of the sonatas, and will be related in connection with the
" Appassionata " sonata.

In spite of everything Beethoven and the Prince were again
reconciled, the Prince living until 1814. He had before then
had occasion to show his readiness to support Beethoven, by
securing him an annuity of 600 florins; and just at the time
when the " Sonata Pathétique " was published, he presented
the Master with a set of the genuine old Italian instruments
for a string quartet, many of Beethoven's chamber music
works being created in his house with the young Schuppanzigh
as leader.

    *   *   *   *   *   *

The two following sonatas, Opus 14, No. 1 in E and No. 2 in
G, are contrasts to Opus 13 in so far as Beethoven in them quite
forsakes the somewhat rhetorical pathetic language which he
had used in the C minor sonata while under the influence of the
antique style. Here he speaks to us in quiet intimacy, as though
sitting down beside us; in the *Allegretto* (E minor) his deeply
moved talk becomes so alive that one can almost imagine
the words underlying it; its leading theme has something of
the character of the *Lied* in its expressiveness. Schindler has
pointed out that Beethoven played the leading subject with a
kind of furious violence, until he reached the " chord " (*i.e.*
the *fermato*), on which he *dwelt very long*, while the *Maggiore*
was played more calmly and quietly and with extraordinarily
beautiful gradations of tone. Here again is one of those
peculiar middle movements in which Beethoven shows how
he can make the piano " speak " in a way it had never spoken

before, and which he employs instead of the *Scherzo* only in the smaller, more intimate sonata, never in the symphonies, thus showing a delicate sense of proportion, not always possessed by the composers of the later romantic school. Above one of his " Bagatelles," Opus 33, Beethoven has written, *con una certa espressione parlante*—words that might also have been written above this *Allegretto.*

While the features of the E major sonata, apart from the passionate fervour of the *Allegretto*, are grace and tenderness, mild radiance without any brilliance or display, the other sonata is swayed rather by caprice. The character of the first movement is almost childlike in its simplicity—and apparently thrown off in a happy mood, but the sure hand of the young Master is revealed in the clearly defined form and in the manner in which the first theme seems of itself to glide over into the second, yet showing a clear and deliberate contrast between the two. Schindler speaks of a strife between two principles in these sonatas, the one beseeching, the other resisting, but we have heard of something like this in the other sonatas, and it may indeed be said of several of Beethoven's greater works, for if it means anything, it indicates a peculiarity of style in his music in general and does not particularly concern this sonata, of which the chief feature, as said before, is its humour. It flourishes and sparkles, though in varying degree and form, not only in the first movement, but also in the *Finale*, which is exceptionally and somewhat loosely called *Scherzo*—for it is not a question of a real *Scherzo*, with a trio, according to the traditional pattern—and in the *Andante* with variations as well, right to the end of the latter, with its *pp* and *ff* boldly and merrily set up against each other. The *staccato* plan of the *Andante* itself might very well be a youthful, merry and playful protest against those who expected from the slow movement only sweet, visionary melodies, and a revelling in their tunefulness.

These two sonatas are dedicated to Baroness von Braun, who must not be confused with the Countess Browne mentioned before. She was married to a man of affairs who had been created a baron, Peter von Braun, who for some years had been theatre director or manager, and about whom opinions vary a good deal. It was he who later on induced Beethoven to compose " Fidelio," and so far the sonatas point onward to a rather storm-tossed part of Beethoven's life : his appearance as an opera-composer with the annoyances and disappointments it brought him. With the " Fidelio " failure in 1806 the good relations between Beethoven and the Brauns seem to have come to an end. Like most of the people with whom we become acquainted through Beethoven's dedications, they were great lovers of music, not only the Baroness, but also her husband, who is even said to have composed music of " sound quality," incidentally the music of Bürger's *Leonore* being his work. There is hardly any connection to be found, though, between the themes of the sonatas and the lady to whom they were dedicated. It is a dedication of courtesy—perhaps a wise one—to the wife of a wealthy baron interested in the fine arts. Meanwhile it is known of this lady that she belonged to that set in Vienna which had a craze for the antique, this finding one of its outlets in the arrangement of her garden, and we may therefore believe that Beethoven, whose interest went in the same direction, would enjoy wandering about amongst its statues and idyllic groves ingeniously copied from those of ancient Greece or Rome.

*   *   *   *   *   *

We have considered before the appreciable contrast between the " Sonata Pathétique " and the two sonatas of Opus 14, between the broad and more outward form of expression and the intimate, rather reticent one. This touches a point in the history of the sonatas on which it is worth while dwelling a little. Hitherto these piano sonatas had occupied a prominent, almost a commanding place in Beethoven's production. Standing beside them, in a chronological sense (the official opus numbers cannot be taken as reliable in regard to the time when Beethoven's works were written), there are other works for piano, especially variations, one of his favourite forms, as we know, also some vocal pieces and chamber music. There are, comparatively speaking, few orchestral works, and in view of the way in which Beethoven was introduced into the musical life of Vienna this is easily understood. It was as a pianist, and especially as one who performed his own compositions, that he was received and appreciated in wealthy and aristocratic *salons*.

But now—about the year 1800—there is a change. Beethoven's position as an artist is now firmly established, he feels that he has the power to achieve greater things, and he does not care so much now about playing to wealthy and aristocratic audiences; he turns, in works on a large scale, in symphonies and piano concertos, to a wider audience, to the larger and more mixed world of the concert-room. One may say with Paul Bekker, though it is perhaps rather one-sided and paradoxical, that Beethoven's art, after being exclusively aristocratic, becomes more democratic. These instrumental works, from their very demands on orchestral equipment, are planned for other surroundings than those of even the largest *salons* of the Austrian magnates, for which Haydn for a long time planned and wrote his symphonies. In their subject-matter and construction these works were written with a view to winning, not a restricted number of connoisseurs, but the sympathy and understanding of the entire musical public of Vienna.

This change of front from *salon* to concert-room can be traced in the piano sonatas. For a long while Beethoven was still faithful to his favourite instrument—indeed, during the years 1800–6 the sonatas follow each other at but short intervals,

E

sometimes even several in the same year. But these sonatas, written at about the same time as the piano sonatas, the C minor concerto, the second symphony and the "Eroica," the first string quartet opus, etc., seem to divide into two directions, according to their form and the ideas contained in them. We get sonatas which, with their broad construction, splendid execution, technical brilliance, with sometimes even the Cadenza of the piano concerto, and with the various prescribed parts in the well-known sequence, seem to turn to the large public of the concert-room, and, on the other hand, sonatas in which Beethoven has taken the piano into his intimate confidence, in the conscious or unconscious need of turning his back on the brilliantly-lit concert-room, in order to interpret within the four walls of his own room, or in the circle of a few understanding friends, what he has at heart, or at any rate something that is not meant for the great and profane assembly which the concert-room has casually gathered in. In sonatas like these he does not feel himself strictly bound by tradition or forms that have been handed down; hence the suggestive title above two of these sonatas : "Quasi una fantasia," while a sonata of the other kind may just as characteristically be called "Grande Sonate."

Now, of course, we cannot venture to say, of the contrast between the style and character of these sonatas, that Beethoven in an individual case was choosing one of the two directions. At the moment when the idea for them took shape, the musical subject, not the thought of the place where they would be performed, would be uppermost in his mind.

And even if it seems that a sonata, judging from the character of its fundamental themes, must be placed in one or the other of these two groups, it may be difficult, owing to its musical working-out, to classify it definitely as a concert-work or unconditionally as an intimate one, yet in the main outlines it is possible to adhere to this division in the attitude and subject-matter of the sonatas. Amongst those essentially

in concert style may be reckoned such sonatas as Opus 22 in
B flat major, Opus 31, No. 2 in D minor, Opus 53 in C
major, Opus 57 in F minor, and standing in the first rank as
their contrast, Opus 27, No. 1 in E flat major, Opus 31, No. 3
in E flat major, Opus 54 in F major, Opus 78 in F sharp
major; in the same group one will also place Opus 27, No. 2
from its entire mood and spiritual idea, even though the
Finale bears the mark of the hand that wrote the piano
concertos.

The remainder of the sonatas form an intermediate group
(before Opus 90). Those most approaching the concert style
seem to be the A flat major Opus 26 (in spite of the free placing
of the movements), the D major Opus 28, the G major Opus 31,
No. 1, and E flat major Opus 81. (The small sonatas or the
sonatinas Opus 49 and 79 may, of course, be disregarded in
this connection.)

Opus 81, the " Lebewohl " sonata, brings us to 1809; in the
same year the piano concerto in E flat major was published, and
this is the last of the piano as a concert instrument.

*   *   *   *   *   *

After this hurried glance over the succession of sonatas in
the decade 1799–1809 we return to our contemplation of the
individual sonatas in their chronological order.

The sonata Opus 22 in B flat major has been called by
Beethoven himself a " *Grande Sonate*," and he sends it to the
publisher, Hoffmeister, with the words : " This sonata is a
corker, my dear fellow " (" hat sich gewaschen ") ! The
Master's satisfaction at a task well accomplished beams from
the jovial remark—and yet his modest claim on the publisher
was only twenty ducats for this sonata, which, as he added,
" will command a bigger sale than both the larger works offered
put together " (*i.e.* Symphony No. 1 and the Septet).

With its four great movements, boldly swung passages, its
brilliant runs and rolling tremolos, Beethoven would consider
this sonata a tit-bit for a pianist—and every artist-pianist will

agree with him. The character of this sonata, its bright, manly tone, its clearness, its dauntless and broad B flat attack, place it as a matter of course amongst the concert sonatas. Yet a Beethoven would not have written it if it did not contain more pondering, brooding parts, such as, in particular, the modulatory part of the first movement, in which the Master, in the course of the development of the theme, engages in all sorts of modulatory twists and turns, called " bold " at that time, apparently, as it had been said, " placing the harmonic element above the melodic."

In the *Adagio* the romantic sounds of a hunter's horn and the dreamy moods of forest glades alternate with the splendours of concert bravura. Beethoven directs it to be performed *con molt' espressione*. Is this because he feels there is an inner lack of this in the music ? For a Beethoven *Adagio* one would scarcely say that this movement is profound or charged with strong personal feeling. The same is true of the little *Menuetto* with the secondary minor movement. The *Finale*, too, is mostly a sonorous piece, a graceful rondo rich in pianistic brilliance and effects, and in variety of theme; now and then, as in the minor sections, a warmer and somehow more personal feeling seems to emerge. The inventiveness with which the leading theme, every time it returns, is introduced in a new way can be traced back to Haydn, but Beethoven has developed what he inherited further with great energy and ingenuity. W. Nagel has pointed out a resemblance that is not slight between the first theme of the *Finale* and the leading subject in a B flat sonata by Ernst W. Wolf (1735–92), a Vienna composer who was very much in favour at that time :

PRINCE CARL LICHNOWSKY.

and thinks that Beethoven was probably acquainted with Wolf's sonata, so that the resemblance is not accidental. Meanwhile, as he adds that there is no other resemblance between the two movements, one is probably quite safe in disregarding the passing agreement. There is all the less reason to set up this hunt for " resemblances " between the Beethoven sonatas and other earlier or contemporary ones—and they have been disregarded in the present work—as certain themes in those days might be called common property, and the composers did not exactly suffer from an overweening desire to be original in this respect, nor did Beethoven in his earlier years. It was not always in the invention of the theme itself, but in its treatment and working-out, that genius and art might be displayed.

One-sided critics of the B flat sonata, like Lenz and Marx, have not had too much difficulty in maintaining that in this instance Beethoven had not given much of his personality, and that in the virtuoso element he had got so much out of his depth, that it appeared to be an end in itself. When, however, the sonata is justly regarded from the point of view of concert-work, there is hardly any reason to quarrel with its creator. Besides, it is certainly harsh and unfair to say that if Beethoven had continued along the same road on which he was then going he would have ended as a second Hummel. It is a comfort, at any rate, that he did not remain on that road! No one has ever dared to depreciate the technical bravura in the C sharp minor sonata, in the so-called " Waldstein " or in the F minor sonata, as serving virtuoso objects *à la Hummel!*

The sonata Opus 22, which was published in 1802, was no doubt already composed in 1800, that is to say, at the same time as such comprehensive works as the first symphony, the Oratorio *Christ on the Mount of Olives*, the C minor piano concerto and others. The sonata is dedicated to Count

Browne, to whose beautiful consort the Opus 10 sonatas were dedicated. That this sonata of Beethoven was one of those most in favour and most frequently performed for a long while, is easily understood, in view of its character and the prevailing taste of that time.

CHAPTER VI

THE sonata Opus 26 in A flat major is remarkable already in its exterior form : it contains four freely arranged parts, one of which, on account of its character, had not previously been considered suitable to a sonata. It begins with a set of variations followed by a *Scherzo*, after which comes the innovation (and the only one in Beethoven's sonatas) : a funeral march, described in Italian as *Marcia funebre sulla Morte d'un Eroe ;* the last movement consists of a short *Allegro*. Here the usual sonata scheme to which Beethoven had hitherto kept is not only abandoned, but the logical connection between the individual parts seems to be very loose, or at least difficult to point out. There is some justification for calling this sonata a forerunner of the two " Quasi fantasia " sonatas of the next Opus ; in a certain sense this sonata, especially its funeral march in A flat minor, can, from the point of view of form, be called even more " fantastic " than the two that follow it.

In itself there is nothing new in beginning a sonata with a set of variations ; perhaps one may even venture to assume that Mozart's famous A major sonata had inspired Beethoven to begin in a similar manner. It is worth noticing that he introduced variations just at this time, because he was now particularly interested in this form of art, in which he displayed great skill and inventiveness. About the year 1800 he wrote several works with variations and he was aware himself that in this field also he had created something new. In a letter to Breitkopf and Härtel (of 1802) he writes the following lines, significant in his psychology as a musician, as he mentions two works with variations which he has planned : " They are both treated in a really new manner, and each in its own way. I assure you that you will not regret these two works ; each theme is treated by itself in a manner different from the others. *Usually I only hear it from others when I have new ideas, as I am never aware of it myself, but this time I do assure you that the style in both is quite new and my own.*" Spontaneousness and simplicity, as well as the self-consciousness of genius, speak from these lines.

The variation movement of the A flat sonata shows to what the Master refers. While Mozart weaves his A major variations round his theme and enriches it with greater and greater brilliance and ornament, Beethoven takes another course, so that we do not see what there really is in the theme until we meet it in the variations. In regard to this movement a writer has expressed it thus : The early composers started from within and worked outwards ; while Beethoven, beginning from without, penetrates into the soul of the theme. Reinecke draws our attention to the fact that these variations will fill their place as the first part of the sonata when they are played without perceptible pauses and all in about the same *tempo*, and Riemann adds that this *tempo* ought preferably to be a graceful Tempo di Menuetto.

Commentatiuncula—in usum Delphini is the title given by Friederich Rochlitz to a delightfully wordy series of comments on these variations. Rochlitz was one of the most prominent Beethoven enthusiasts of the day, and valued by the composer himself as an æsthete and poet. These comments on the variations are to be found in Rochlitz's periodical *Für Freunde der Tonkunst*, and appear as though written by an elderly lawyer's clerk from the remoter part of Pomerania (in 1806, that is, a year after the publication of the sonata). In the original review these " Comments " take up 28 pages, and only a few short extracts can be given here—not only for the sake of their quaintness (and because only few readers of these pages will have easy access to Rochlitz's review), but in order to show how commonplace and prosy, how soberly and " respectably," even one who valued Beethoven's work highly, and thought he understood it, could think of " commenting " upon his music. Even though it may have been his intention to give a humorous or ironical picture of the supposed " commentator," this does not distinctly appear.

The author makes the worthy old clerk recognise all his own (very commonplace) life in the Beethoven variations, its exterior events and the emotions they have produced in himself. As an example of how he does this, and of the prevalent tone of the Beethoven interpretations of the time, a few fragments are given below :

" *Theme* : The subject is given, the foundation, which is to be further developed. A flat ; 3/4 time, serious rather than cheerful, yet gentle, kindly and pleasant ; moreover, not lacking in strength and very promising in a modest way. Now look here, Bernhard, I said to myself : It was just like that, *your* foundation, that God had given you, that had to be further developed. . . . Yes, thus did your Creator equip you, and how great was His mercy ! Thus did your stern father support you and your devout mother nourish you, in body and mind—and how lovingly ! Well, well, it was not much, but it was good and it was *your* fundamental theme. Now let us ask : What has it become ? Beethoven's variations answer clearly.

" *Variatio I.* There is a theme, to be sure, but it is dissolved in figures constantly changing, sunk into the depths and driven up on the heights. I had reached boyhood and been placed in the grammar school—the theme was there, but dissolved in figures which looked quite different. The good foundation was split up, scattered, torn in pieces above and below. . . .

"*Variatio II*. Look, here is the theme again ! gallant and splendid in the bass ! Ah, yes, it is myself, as though he had stolen my face out of the looking-glass . . . I had grown up, I was attending the University. The life of freedom and independence, new to me, strengthened me and bore me up ; but a monstrous conceit, pride and defiance took possession of me.

"*Variatio III*. Heavy and melancholy, sad, as it were downcast, this variation seems to move onward only with difficulty . . . at length dying away dully under the burden of its many flats : A flat minor ! " (The explanation that follows this, of the meaning of the seven flats in Bernhard's life : poverty, poor examination result, failure of literary attempts, etc., etc., is delightful to the verge of the grotesque, but cannot be quoted further here.)

"*Variatio IV*. That was my state during the next three weeks. There is hardly a word to be added to it. Outwardly I was completely apathetic ; but my strength worked all the harder from within." . . . (Strange, that this Scherzo-like variation should be considered apathetic !)

"*Variatio V*. . . . It has a confiding, mobile character : both hands have plenty to do, and what they have to do is closely connected. And what is the main thing ? You have only to look at the notes. After a short encouraging prelude." (evidently Rochlitz had not discovered the half-hidden theme in the chain of triplets) " the fundamental theme follows note by note, in spite of all that has happened in between . . . line upon line the state is described there which has been the prevailing one with me for close upon fifty years. I realised what my innocently happy, humble childhood had been, first in imagination, finally in being and doing. I saw now that the first fundamental theme was not lost to me after all. It came back again, note by note—and yet, how different !" (All as in Beethoven's music.)

As in a flash these well-meant, tedious and diluted comments on the variations show us what a gulf there was between the young genius and the time in which he lived, and which he had left far behind him !—

The Scherzo movement is clear and concise, and typical of Beethoven at this period. There is a gentle, dreamy poetry in the Trio, the expression of which points onward to the piano style of Robert Schumann, of whom there is also a suggestion in the fourth variation. On the other hand, a passage in the *Scherzo* foretells a corresponding place in the fifth, C minor symphony, of which we are again reminded in the fifth variation, where the melody in the middle voice is woven into and adorned by agitated figuration. Altogether it will be interesting to look in the piano sonatas for instances of forerunners of the great instrumental works. It is quite natural that the works written in the lesser compass which is more easily surveyed should contain ideas which can be found again, used in a deeper form under larger conditions.

The " Funeral March " above all has made this sonata famous. It is said by Beethoven's pupil, Ferdinand Ries, to have been inspired by an opera by Paër,* but this is rather improbable as the sketch of the sonata Opus 26 was begun before Paër's opera *Achilles* was produced in Vienna, on which occasion a funeral march certainly was a conspicuous success. The din of battle, the clash of arms, the deaths that Europe had seen of so many heroes, might well quicken Beethoven's imagination and appeal to his artist's soul with its particular susceptibilities to political events (apart from an Italian opera on a Viennese stage). The idea for the funeral march is evidently conceived as a piece of music for a military orchestra ; we recognise at the piano not only the various wind instruments,

---

* Ferdinando Paër (1771–1839), an Italian composer much in favour at that time, the writer of numerous melodious operas, settled in Vienna in 1797 and remained there for some years. With his *Leonora* he was, by the way, to cross Beethoven's path later as an opera composer. According to an equally doubtful tradition the rumour of Admiral Nelson's death (at Aboukir) is said to have inspired Beethoven with the idea of the funeral march.

but also the mournful rolling of the kettledrums. For we are present at the obsequies of a fallen hero. In so far we again have before us a precursor of a greater instrumental work : the funeral march in the " Eroica " symphony, but if we listen more closely we become aware of the difference. Here we encounter mostly the external, mournful pomp—only the burial is presented to our view. In the " Eroica " there is a deeper vision ; there the whole tragic fate of the hero is brought before our minds by the tones of the funeral march.

It cannot be denied that the smoothly flowing final movement, flexible and lightly emotional, accords strangely with the gloom of the funeral march. It is difficult to find any connection between the two pieces, unless one would perceive fleeting shadows of the funeral march in the scattered minor passages falling on the bright major movement. The latter, which is most like a Rondo (and somewhat like a study in its bearing), is said by Czerny to have been inspired by corresponding pieces in Cramer's sonatas, especially an A flat major movement, which really has some external resemblance to that of Beethoven's work in more than the key, and this opinion is supported by Beethoven experts. But in that case Beethoven has certainly ennobled and enriched what he may possibly have borrowed from Cramer. One may probably venture to suppose that this movement did not mean more to him than a vivacious pianistic close of a sonata, in which it was necessary to efface or soften the mournful impression of the funeral march. In that case it seems to be taking matters *too* solemnly—as some have wanted to do—to comment upon it with quotations from Beethoven's letters at this time, such as these : " Every day I come nearer to the goal which I feel but cannot describe : resting is out of the question," or, " A quiet life, no, I feel that I am not made for that."

The A flat major sonata is dedicated to the Prince Carl Lichnowsky mentioned above, and therefore dates from a time when the relations between the composer and his patron were

FACSIMILE OF A PORTION OF THE MS. OF THE A FLAT MAJOR SONATA
(Op. 26).

FACSIMILE OF A PORTION OF THE MS. OF THE SONATA IN A (Op. 101).

at their best; probably it was performed for the first time by Beethoven in the usual circle. One would presume it to be one of the works resulting from occasions when the composer played improvisations on the piano to such audiences as these, but we have no definite information on the subject. The sonata was published in March 1802 and was announced as a " Grande Sonate." Perhaps this title was given by the publisher, but no doubt with Beethoven's approval, and, as indicated above, the sonata belongs mainly to those meant for the concert-room. In the sketch-book it is, as a rule, called " Sonata pour M." or " für M." It is not known who is meant by this; but it looks as though the work was originally intended for someone other than the Prince; and that the changes in Beethoven's moods, which were not rare, caused him to alter his decision in favour of Prince Lichnowsky. The funeral march is sure to have created a great sensation, especially when interpreted by the master hand of Beethoven himself. It could be understood at once by all, and on everyone it must have made a deep impression. The aristocratic ladies would again surround and admire the young genius, his performance, and the beautiful brow from which such a work of art had sprung. Perhaps it was on an occasion like this that Beethoven answered a lady who could not restrain her languishing admiration for this brow, in these words, " Kiss it then, since it is so beautiful!"

*   *   *   *   *   *

There is a handsome facsimile edition of this sonata from Beethoven's manuscript (Fr. Cohn, Publisher, Bonn, 1895), printed at the instance of the late Erich Prieger, a wealthy amateur and musical scholar. A page of this MS. is given facing page 60, as a life-like impression of Beethoven's music handwriting. This edition is also interesting in not *quite* agreeing with the editions of the sonata generally published. The difference is not seen in the most important part, the actual notes, yet there is one thing which was far from unim- portant to the Master: the expression signs. They differ slightly in the way in which they are employed from those we find in the ordinary printed editions. This raises the question : were these alterations made by Beethoven himself when reading the proof-sheets of the sonata ? It would seem probable, especially as we have instances in which the Master elsewhere corrected his work up to the last, even when in the printer's hands; the sonata Opus 106 (*Adagio*) is a famous example of this and will be dealt with in its own place. The further question, then, is : Do the corrected proofs of Beethoven's works exist, and, so far as we are concerned, those of his piano works, as these proof-sheets—the most authentic witnesses of Beethoven's thoughts—would often be of great interest ?

So far as we know, the Beethoven literature, though it is immense, contains nothing that might enlighten us on this point. The present writer therefore made inquiries of two authorities of the first rank in musical research in Germany, Professor Dr. Max Friedländer and Professor Dr. Max Seiffert. Unfortunately the result was negative. The two music historians were unable to throw any light on the subject; but they were both of opinion that the proof-sheets in question must unfortunately be presumed to have been destroyed, and so irrecoverably lost. Max Friedländer writes on this matter : " Druckabzüge von Beethovenschen Werken mit eigenhändigen Korrekturen des Meisters bisher so gut wie niemals bekannt worden sind. Aehnliches trifft leider, leider auch auf die Werke Haydns, Mozarts, Schuberts und vieler andern Komponisten zu. Es gehörte eben zu den üblen Traditionen der Vorleger solche Korrekturabzüge einfach zu vernichten." *

---

* " Prints of Beethoven's works with corrections in his own handwriting have so far hardly ever been published. This is unfortunately also true of the works of Haydn, Mozart, Schubert and many other composers. There is even a bad tradition amongst publishers, following which rough-proofs were simply destroyed."—Tr.

CHAPTER VII

THE names of two ladies of the great world of Vienna are bound up with Beethoven's Opus 27, which consists of two sonatas, the " Fantasia " sonatas in E flat major and C sharp minor. This is explained by the fact that the sonatas originally appeared separately, each with its own dedication. The first dedication, of the E flat sonata, to Signora Principessa Giovanni Lichtenstein, does not convey much, beyond a token of courtesy on the part of the composer towards a musically interested relative of his benefactor in the early days at Bonn, Count Waldstein. We know but little of any further connection between Beethoven and the Princess, still less of that between the music and the dedication, and nothing can be gathered from the work itself.

Like its sister sonata in C sharp minor, this one begins with a movement (*Andante*) which is not in the traditional form, and which, even in the description—*quasi una fantasia*—is a peculiarly constructed piece, the E flat major section of which breathes forth a strange joy of the soul; its delicate tone is characterised by the frequent *p* and *pp*. If one tries to find a spiritual connection between this piece and the conditions of life in which it arose together with the C sharp minor sonata in 1801 (published 1802), one is involuntarily led to think of a gentle dream of mutual love. The form is that of the *Lied*, a single phrase, the most heartfelt in the whole movement, sings out all its depth of feeling, and occurs only once, as though timidly fearing to repeat this outburst. At the same time this shows a prodigality not usual in a Beethoven composition, as the phrase is not worked out, indeed the composer does not return to it in the whole course of the *Andante*.

This movement has been found insignificant, not quite worthy of Beethoven (Lenz, Elterlein), and according to Riemann this is due to the first, somewhat stiff theme, which has even been called "commonplace." In Beethoven's defence, Riemann maintains that the fault lies with the reader of the theme, as it looks when read straight from Beethoven's writing of it.

In order to rescue it from triviality and endow it with "an attraction even particularly intimate," Riemann would read it thus :

Now this is bound up with the whole of Riemann's peculiar "method of phrasing," the discussion of which is outside the scope of these pages. But is there really any doubt that Beethoven thought and felt the theme in the sense in which he wrote it, and that he did not feel it to be a triviality, such as it appears in the accompanying bass figure ? In the very next section it is already difficult to understand the same theme in Riemann's sense, and to Beethoven the two sections must have been rhythmically identical. Nor does the re-shaping of the theme in the fourth section as Beethoven writes it :

seem to support Riemann's view.

Against the gentle, scarcely breathed E flat section, there is another, more "earthly" one in C major. With its easy flight in the beginning it *may* well be interpreted—as indeed it has been—as a triumphant feeling of happiness and thus be understood as a fresh expression of amorous feelings ; but this

GIULIETTA GUICCIARDI.

BEETHOVEN (c. 1801).

somewhat study-like section does not seem to be particularly inspired.

The second movement is a *Scherzo* in the true Beethoven manner, with all its wealth of rhythmic inventiveness, of mysterious elfin mood and radiant humour. This is followed —without any intervening pause, as Beethoven expressly wishes it, probably in agreement with the fantasia-character of the sonata—by an equally Beethovenesque *Adagio*. This is again a kind of *Lied*, wistful and sad, but harmonious and clear as the day. The immediate impression is that of a slow and independent movement, but its dreaming is suddenly broken off by the buoyant vivacity of the *Finale*, in which the *Adagio* again appears as a memory towards the end of the sonata. As Riemann has aptly said, the *Finale* is made up of a number of tiny stones into a dainty mosaic. The roots of its second subject go so far back as the Bonn quartet that was the foundation of the first movement in the C major sonata, Opus 2 ! There is really no melodic development in this movement, and in its gay transparency one is more aware of the sparkling play of sound and the unerring hand of the Master than of any message from his soul.

The unity which is a feature of the C sharp minor sonata, and raises it to such an exalted position, will be sought for in vain in this sister sonata in E flat, nor has this the depth and richness of poetic feeling of the former. Regarded as a whole, the impression given by this sonata is rather that of a certain unrest, as an experimental attempt to find a new form of expression.

*　　*　　*　　*　　*　　*

The second sonata, in C sharp minor, takes us at one stroke into Beethoven's love story. The music speaks loudly of it, and from other sources we can, at any rate to a certain extent, supply the missing details of what it tells us : the sonata is dedicated to Damigella Contessa Giulietta Guicciardi, and

F

Beethoven's relations with this young Italian countess can even be elucidated by his own words.

Two well-known statements about this love of Beethoven's have been preserved. One depicts him as having a chaste nature, far removed from sensual passion, which was even unknown to it. Seyfried writes : " Strange to say, Beethoven never had a love affair." The other statement is a flat contradiction of the first : " Beethoven was always in love with someone, and as a rule in a violent degree." These words are Wegeler's, and he claims as witnesses Stephan Breuning, Ferdinand Ries and other friends. The latter statement is doubtless nearest the truth, but in the main as little is known of the objects of Beethoven's affections as of the nature of the Master's feelings.

It has been said in an earlier chapter that he seems to have passed through a Werther period with its too sensitive dreaming, but it is quite certain that his heart was not altogether and everywhere dominated by feelings of this kind. It has been said elsewhere of his love affairs that they seldom absorbed him for very long, and according to the few and scattered accounts available, some of them were of a transient and not exactly hallowed character. These women quickly passed before his view ; for a shorter or longer while he would extract some pleasure from being with them, and allow it to inspire his artist's imagination, yet they seem to have left no deeper impression or lasting memory in his mind. At times he would seek and find women friends in the aristocratic circles in Vienna, into which he was introduced early in his life. Whether his relations with them were platonic and visionary or whether his affections were really involved, it is impossible to say now. We only know that Beethoven was fêted to the point of hysteria by these ladies. At other times he found them in a lower sphere : thus Ferdinand Ries once surprised Beethoven in ardent talk with a young and beautiful lady, for whose forgiveness the composer was fervently pleading, and at Beethoven's express desire Ries had to accompany the conversation with improvisations on the piano! It turned out that the young Master did not know even the lady's name or her position (if he did not deliberately conceal his knowledge!), and Ries accidentally found out later that she was the mistress of one of the foreign ambassadors.—Beethoven had a quarrel with the English violinist Bridgetower (a mulatto) about " a girl," and this cost his rival the dedication of the violin sonata which has now become famous under the name of Rudolph Kreutzer. Ries, again, relates that while he was lodging in the house of a tailor with three extremely pretty daughters, his great Master visited him very frequently! There are some indications then, that his ardent temperament was at times not very fastidious in regard to amorous affairs. This light view of the passion of love accords well enough with the spirit of the time, which on the whole did not take a sentimental or serious view of the relations between men and women. And though Beethoven's genius soared to great heights above temporal things, in many human ways he was and could not help being a child of the age. Yet one need only quote a single one of Beethoven's free-spoken utterances to feel how remote he is from the mere love of pleasure without any deeper feelings, characteristic of this period. He says : " Sensual pleasure without union of the souls is and always will be an animal one, it leaves behind no noble feelings whatever, only remorse." One feels, though, that he speaks about this remorse from experience.

Nor is there any doubt that Beethoven had a visionary feminine ideal. From his letters and the tone poetry of his " Fidelio " it is clear that he had his dreams of marriage and saw its deep moral significance for man and woman.

Now Beethoven's relations with Giulietta Guicciardi are amongst those of which we know a little more than the others. This young Italian girl, who was of a noble family, came with her parents to Vienna from Trieste, and Beethoven met her at the house of her relatives, the Brunswicks. She became his pupil in piano playing and remained so for at any rate about two years. His interest was quickly aroused in this young Italian beauty, who was only about sixteen or seventeen years old; about her expressive features, it has been said, there was often a tinge of melancholy.* Mutual feelings soon arose. What this meant to Beethoven can be seen in his letter to Wegeler of November 1801, in which he writes that after having been a misanthropist, he has now become sociable, and that this change has been caused by " a dear, charming girl, who loves me, and whom I love. I feel for the first time that marriage might make me happy. . . . Unfortunately she is not of my station—and anyhow I could not marry at present; I must still see a good deal more of life."

What do these words mean? And what were Giulietta's feelings? Was she only a forward little flirt, slightly in love with and enraptured by the great Master; flattered by his attentions, which he would hardly attempt to conceal in the presence of her aristocratic relatives? And did Beethoven at an early stage suspect this? Or was it Giulietta, who had an inkling that she was, after all, only for a time Beethoven's " flame "—the slang term in those Viennese sets for Beethoven's love affairs—who could for the present " inspire " him? Or did she, or perhaps rather her parents as practical Italians, soon begin to think of more substantial prospects for her future? No definite material giving the answer to these questions has been handed down to us. All the sentiment that has been wrapped round this relationship is of no real value.

Nor, in spite of countless writings, has an absolute and definite decision been arrived at as to whether that famous Beethoven letter which is called, from an expression used in it,

* The picture given here, probably the only one in existence, and far from distinguished, does not seem to give one much idea of her appearance.

" to the immortally beloved " (die unsterbliche Geliebte), is written to Giulietta Guicciardi or to someone else.

The letter, which was found amongst Beethoven's effects, was written in pencil, in three parts, each with its own date, but without mention of the year. It is a beautiful, poetic piece of writing, the outburst of a storm-tossed mind, after the manner of Werther's notes, more poetic, more literary in form than Beethoven's other letters, about the form of which he was, as a rule, not much concerned. Beethoven was not and did not wish to be a writer in the same sense as later musicians, such as Weber, Schumann and Wagner, except in this one instance in which he was more than a writer, in fact a poet. The highly-strung rhapsodic air of this letter seems in a way to remind one of the accounts we have of Beethoven's improvisations and *ex tempore* fantasias at the piano.

The letter seems never to have been sent ; at any rate nothing is known about it. It can hardly have been sent in the form in which it was left by Beethoven, but, as we see, he kept the letter as a treasure in a secret drawer of his writing-table. The faded paper fell out when his relatives, the instant he had closed his eyes in death, instituted a ghoulish hunt for papers of value which the ageing, suspicious and close-handed Beethoven kept in the same secret drawer. A proof of what this letter meant to him !

The contention about this letter has set many pens in motion ; it has even produced a forged letter, which has been published as a continuation of the genuine one. The main object of this strife has been to prove that A. Schindler was wrong in designating Giulietta Guicciardi as " the immortally beloved." Who the latter was, in that case, has been a matter of great dispute among the learned, who have fought manfully about it. Theresa Brunswick, her sister Josephine, afterwards Countess Deym, Marianna Willmann, Bettina Brentano, Amalie Sebald and perhaps others have each had their own champion.

The best equipped of these knights is the American, Thayer,
author of the great Beethoven biography, who was the first to
pull the wreath from Giulietta's dusky locks in order to place
them on the not quite so beautiful ones of Theresa Brunswick.
Yet this victory was not final, but most students now seem to
be uncertain or to have given up trying to solve the problem.—
Now, if, instead of following a precedent and studying old
almanacks, lists of travellers, of visitors at watering-places and
visitors' books, and undertaking other praiseworthy and tiresome labour of this kind, one simply keeps to the letter (or the
draft of the letter) as it has been found, its contents and its
appearance, there still seems to be something to support the
sharply contested view of Schindler, that is, that the letter was
intended for Giulietta.   First of all there is this point : that
the C sharp minor sonata, which was dedicated to Giulietta in
1801, speaks the very same undulating, rapt, pain-filled language
as the letter ; while the F sharp major sonata, Opus 78, dedicated to Theresa Brunswick in 1810, is written in quite
another, placid, gently graceful style, as elaborate as filigree
work ; there is not a hint in it of a passionately perturbed mind,
unhappy or blissful.

Further, the whole style of the letter is much more like that
of a young man of about thirty than of one who has advanced
ten years further on the road of life.

Finally, it seems—a point which has, strange to say, been
missed by the large number of students of this subject—that
the very appearance of this piece of writing is in favour of its
having been written at an earlier date.   This is a point on which
experts in handwriting should be able to express an exact
and definite opinion ; but everyone who has a slight acquaintance with Beethoven's life and person knows that his handwriting, which was certainly never beautiful nor legible—it
was characteristic of a genius !—in the course of time became
more and more " wild," " unrestrained," regardless of form

and line, and to an unpractised eye often quite unreadable. In this letter, however, the writing is in the beginning—for a Beethoven—quite clear, careful, almost dainty and not difficult to read. A handwriting expert would quite certainly not attribute the first pages to Beethoven's later years. It is true that this " distinct " writing ceases on the next pages of the letter. As the mood grows upon him, as the blood courses more quickly through his veins, and he is more violently swayed by his feelings, the next pages, written on two consecutive days, become more and more " Beethoven," and the writing very difficult to decipher. But surely this cannot displace the time when the letter was written; and it seems to be a reasonable explanation that we have before us a draft of a letter (which was perhaps never sent) or possibly even a lyrical effusion in letter form, which was never *intended* to be sent. Beethoven would therefore, soon after the neat beginning, abandon good handwriting and legibility, as after all he was only writing for his own sake, and take the paper into his confidence as he had so often taken the piano. A great deal in this much-discussed document in Beethoven's life seems to support the view that it may date from the same time as the C sharp minor sonata.

Yet, whether the letter was a beautiful poem to the immortally beloved, conceived in lonely dreams of her, and never reaching her, or whether it really was sent, and who the right addressee was in that case, is a question which will probably never be solved.

On the other hand, we stand on firmer ground when we ask about Giulietta's later relations with Beethoven and about her subsequent fate. We know that she abandoned her—more or less deep—love for him, as she married a Count Wenzel von Gallenberg in 1803. In him she had a husband of her own station (cf. Beethoven's letter to Wegeler, mentioned above), and, moreover, one who was a composer into the bargain, though he was only a composer of dance music. Count Gallenberg wrote ballet music and was a theatre contractor. He did not belong to the great—and wealthy—nobility, and he and Giulietta seem to have led a Bohemian sort of life. A few years after the marriage they were in Italy; later the Count (about 1820) had a share in the management of the Court opera together with a well-known impresario named Barbaja. He now and then had business relations with Beethoven, who, however, did not care for him. As director of the Kärntnertor Theatre in Vienna he became bankrupt (1829), again went to Italy as ballet composer and theatre manager, and died in Rome in 1839. Giulietta was not happy with her music Count, but she would probably not have made Beethoven the ideal wife of his dreams. At any rate she developed into something of an adventuress. In Naples she was the mistress of the well-known writer and man of pleasure, Prince Pückler-Muskau; he mentions her, in respectful phrases however, as " the most beautiful woman in Naples." She survived her husband, dying so late as 1856, it is believed in Vienna. Being questioned in her old age about her relations with Beethoven, she answered with reserve, only speaking of him as her tutor, and even then reluctantly, at least without affection or warmth.*

But from Beethoven himself we have a remarkable statement about their mutual relations. He had certainly not forgotten her. In 1823, when Count Gallenberg was director of the Kärntnertor Theatre, A. Schindler was in communication with him on behalf of Beethoven, and this led to a significant conversation in writing between the Master and his " familiar." Beethoven was now totally deaf and writing was his only means of communication with the world around him. These

* The great pianist, Edward Fischer, has related to the author that an old Viennese gentleman once told him about a conversation he had had with the old Countess. On this occasion she spoke of Beethoven as one who had composed some " crazy " music, but in her Viennese manner she added, " But his playing—it was *heavenly* ! " A characteristic statement, which again shows from what angle these circles regarded and admired Beethoven—that is, as a piano virtuoso.

conversations were written down in a book kept for the purpose, and we thus have a written record of the words that were exchanged between Beethoven and Schindler. They seem to have had their " talk " in a public place; for this reason Beethoven—who was growing more and more suspicious—also wrote his *answers*, a thing he very seldom did, and this dialogue therefore possesses a completeness and actuality not otherwise found in the conversation books. Beethoven's answers are given in French; this has been regarded, justly or unjustly, as a further sign of suspicion. May it not have been a remembrance of the language often used by the young Master and his fair pupil ?

Schindler writes (to Beethoven) : He (Gallenberg) did not make me think very highly of him.

Beethoven : I was his unseen benefactor through others. (It is not known what is intended by this remark; probably Beethoven on various occasions induced his influential friends to give the Count financial help for Giulietta's sake, and, thinking of her, he adds :) She cared very much for me, more than she ever did for her husband. He was always my enemy and that was the very reason I did all that I could for him. (A thoroughly " Beethoven " utterance !)

Schindler : That was probably why he said to me, He is an insufferable person !—most likely out of pure gratitude ! Though may the Lord forgive them, for they know not what they do !

Presently the talk turned to the Countess.

Schindler : Was she rich ? Is she still beautiful ? Is it long since she was married to Count Gallenberg ?

Beethoven : Her maiden name was Guicciardi. (These words : *elle était née G.* . . . are written with unusual neatness and distinctness and a curved line is drawn about the whole sentence. This can hardly be called accidental when one knows what this name once meant to Beethoven. It is as though he had dwelt a little on it in the conversation and had drawn a memorial wreath about the name that was once so dear to him.—The beginning of the next sentence, written in the Master's hand, is not easy to decipher—it concludes thus :) When she came back to Vienna, she came to me in tears, but I despised her.

Schindler : Hercules at the parting of the ways !

Beethoven : If I had cared to spend my energies on *such a life* (underlined by Beethoven ; do the words mean " in an unhappy marriage," or " as her lover," which the expression " despised," used immediately before, might suggest ?), what would be left then, for the nobler, the better. . . ?

These are Beethoven's significant, parting words to Giulietta, on whom he had bestowed the C sharp minor sonata !—

If we now turn with this knowledge, fragmentary though it is, to the sonata itself, we shall understand it better, and its deep resigned pain, its turbulent passion, will speak to us more distinctly and impressively than ever. There cannot be any doubt that this music was conceived in deeply stirred hours in the life of the Master, and that it is the spontaneous expression of the pain of a newly inflicted wound, rather than the dwelling on the memories of it in the imagination. Not least is this true of the *Finale*, which rushes on like a storm of passion and speaks an unusually living and " actual " language. A further proof that we have before us an immediate, spontaneous and unreflecting outburst of the soul seems to be indicated by the absence of any sketches for this sonata—in contrast to nearly all the others. It does not seem to have come into existence, like so many earlier and later ones, piece by piece, often at different times, but to have sprung from Beethoven's brain— and heart—in one mighty whole. The fact that it is less " worked-out " (thematically, contrapuntally) than many of the other sonatas, points in the same direction. It is painted *al fresco* in broad, impressive, violent and easily discernible lines.

Some there are who have shrugged their shoulders at the " romance " that has thus been put into the C sharp minor sonata. Yes, that is quite true, one can enjoy the music and feel enriched by it without this—but after all the romance *is* there. Beethoven himself wrote the name " Fantasia " above the sonata, and everyone can and must read the meaning conveyed in it.

But to those who read this tone poem with imagination and understanding, the singular character of the erotic element in it will have a further appeal. The sensuous expression of love as it is often found, for instance, in the music of Mozart and Schubert, is rare in that of Beethoven, but not even this sonata, sprung directly from a love relationship, speaks the language of passion in music. Beethoven, who shunned all loose talk, and condemned it in others, is delicate in not revealing anything about the object of his love. We can at least get a glimpse of Aloysia and Constance in Mozart's music, and Schubert tells us a little here and there about the charming women who ruled his heart, but there is not the slightest hint of Giulietta in the C sharp minor sonata ! It is concerned with Beethoven—with the turmoil of his manly soul, his melancholy and his great struggles. One might say, perhaps, it is concerned with the super-sensuous erotic love of a genius.

The popular and well-known name given later to this sonata was that of the " Moonlight Sonata." Beethoven himself never called it that. The name was given to it by a poetising music-writer named Rellstab, an enthusiast, by the way, in spreading abroad the fame of Beethoven. The first movement reminded him of a moonlight evening at the Lake of Geneva ! that was how people in those days loved to characterise music ; the moonlight name was eagerly seized upon by publishers and printers, and, alas ! to this day it is often put on concert programmes. Undoubtedly the sonata owes no small part of its fame and popularity to this title.

Perhaps it cannot be denied that there is a certain nocturne mood in the *Adagio sostenuto* of the first movement, but in the profound, human subject, manly in its pain, unsentimental in its expression, it is certainly rather far from most music nocturnes. And the following lines will show how far astray this moonlight and nocturne idea can lead a commentator who is both intelligent and well-informed : " The moonlight lies upon the water like a lane of quivering gold, leading on to the land of our dreams. We sit in the boat together, in close embrace, and listen to the murmuring song of the waves as we glide along the golden path, further and further into the unknown land. It cannot be described—we can only listen, only feel . . ." and then there are even (unfortunately) a couple of lines from a verse of Novalis. So far, then, may a false, sentimental title of this sonata lead. Where, in this interpretation, is the lonely Master, sitting with bowed head at the piano and confiding to his instrument his great, deeply breathing elegy ? Where, not least, are the bitter accents that several times break the monotony of the mournful soliloquy ? The movement of this sonata has nothing whatever to do with idylls or sentimentality.

To mention briefly one more commentary of this *Adagio*, there is one which contends that the sonata was inspired by a poem called *Die Beterin* written by Seume, who was not in the first rank of poets. The subject of it, the prayer of a young girl that her father may be restored to health, might possibly have aroused some sympathy in Beethoven, and it is said that he wrote something of the kind to the poet. But the letter, which no longer exists, certainly dates from quite another time, and altogether this commentary looks very improbable.*

This " song without words " might look rather strange, as the first part of a sonata which has not the features of sonata

---

* This popular sonata had still one more name in earlier days : Die Lauben-Sonate (" The leafy sonata "), which, however, only alluded to the arbour in which Beethoven was supposed to have written it !

form, and probably the introduction had no small share in the title " Fantasia " which Beethoven gave to his Opus 27. This introduction is followed by the little *Allegretto*—standing between the melancholy of the *Adagio* and the tumultuous passion of the *Finale* " like a flower between two abysses." That is Liszt's delicately poetical definition of the piece—which, however, does not in any way explain the psychological connection between the three parts of the sonata. The subject of the sonata *is* contained in the *first* and *last* movements, but the work required a contrast, both psychologically and artistically, a centre of calm between the two C sharp minor storms, the one oppressive and the other clamorous. Beethoven purposely calls the movement *Allegretto*, not *Scherzo*, notwithstanding its outer resemblance to the latter form. He cannot and does not wish to provoke any *Scherzo* mood here ; the movement seems rather to be an unassuming, almost anxious attempt to awaken some confidence in a happier destiny, some little hope of interior harmony, but it is only short-lived and the attempt does not succeed. The *Finale* breaks in upon it without a pause, like the beat of a tremendous wave,* sweeping away the gentle D flat, or, if one prefers, the C sharp major mood of the *Allegretto*, and in the last movement of the sonata there is again fought that " fight against fate " so frequent and violent in Beethoven, especially in the years of his manhood.

He does not reach any major close in this work ; pain is still wringing his heart too much, he cannot tear himself from its grasp—cannot, as he said himself, " seize fate by the throat."

---

* The beginning of the *Finale* involuntarily gives the impression of a rising wave, which at its highest part " shows its teeth " and breaks (in the *ff* chords) ; but in Beethoven's directions, the accuracy and carefulness of which are, as a rule, worthy of note and observance, there is no crescendo sign. Moreover, piano virtuosi may be heard performing this part with literal exactness ; the ascending passages *p* and the chords with a sudden, violent force. The former view, however, seems more reasonable and attractive, regarded artistically and psychologically, and the author is able to state with satisfaction than an Anton Rubinstein performed the passages in question in this manner.

One feels again that the experience is too recent—the Master has not reached the lofty detachment of a Goethe. Yet although this stupendous despair demands our deep sympathy we do not hear the wild torrent of sound with disquiet or with oppressed anxiety. For not only is the passion in itself so beautiful and its artistic expression so proudly restrained and manly, but the bright spirit, the melodious flight, and not least the rhythmical power in this piece of music do not leave us in doubt for one moment that the Master will not succumb to his suffering or his grief. Inactive brooding is unknown to him—he will rise hardened, doubly strong through his pain and the artist's fate that has been allotted to him.

Besides, the C sharp minor sonata had to close on the gloomy minor notes by which it is almost wholly dominated. Whether the rupture with the object of his adoration had occurred when he wrote his music about it, or whether he only suspected its near approach, the scorching pain at tearing himself away from her as from a fair hope, a lovely dream, was upon him. What this dream has held the C sharp minor sonata does not tell us, but perhaps, as indicated earlier, we may be allowed to read about it in the first fantasia sonata in E flat major—in any case in its first movement and in the Violin Sonata in F major— about contemporaneous with the sonatas of Opus 27—the so-called " Spring sonata " with its happy, joyous and lively movement. Such a pyschological duality is far from being unique in Beethoven. It has been thought that there is a connection between the C sharp minor sonata and the next one, Opus 28, the " Pastoral Sonata." There are no external proofs to support this view, yet it cannot be rejected altogether as groundless, when one remembers the Master's consoling words in the letter to the " immortally beloved ": " Oh, God ! look out upon the beauty of nature and calm thy mind before that which *must* be so ! "

CHAPTER VIII

THE sonata Opus 28 was written in the same year as the C sharp minor, Beethoven apparently following his usual custom in having both works in hand at the same time. This would also seem to confirm the thought suggested in the previous chapter, that there is a certain interior connection between the two sonatas.

The D major sonata was called the " Pastoral," not by the composer himself, but by the publisher, Cranz, of Hamburg. In this case the title seems to have been a happy choice and a justified advertisement. We really find here a perfectly calm, harmonious and brightly optimistic mood, an even temper, a thankful joy, all of which there is good reason to attribute to Beethoven's marked love of Nature and to his deep, personal enjoyment of it. Even the minor of the *Andante* sings in tones of exalted calm, and soon this slow piece glides into gay, almost playful D major strains, reminding one of the enlivening twitter of birds and effacing the impression of the more serious minor preceding it. When a writer suggests that there is an allegory in this movement, the beasts of the forest following the dead hunter to his last resting-place : the funeral in a minor and the song of birds in a major key, with the joy of the animals that they are safe from their enemy now—one cannot but wonder at the results arrived at by an eager, inventive and " poetic " interpretation of absolute music.*

In the announcements this sonata again was called " Grande Sonate," and, as stated earlier, it must in the main be classed

---

* According to Czerny this was for a long time the Master's favourite piece, which he played often and willingly.

amongst those written for the concert-room.   It is dedicated to Joseph von Sonnenfels, " Conseiller aulique," Secretary to the Academy of Fine Arts.   The dedication does not tell us much.   It seems to have been an act of courtesy towards a man who held a high position in the art world of Vienna, and who would no doubt—elderly and influential as he was—be able to give the comparatively young composer help or support, or perhaps he had shown him understanding, sympathy and interest.   None of the Beethoven biographers seem to know of any closer connection between the two men.   Sonnenfels, a highly gifted man of Jewish family, but himself a Christian, was, however, a prominent personality in Austrian educational schemes, and was occupied particularly in the improvement of scenic art.   It is well known that Beethoven was very interested in and influenced by the humanitarian movement in this age of enlightenment.   Can it have been in this field that the two spirits met ?

The sonata is said to have been composed during one of Beethoven's many sojourns in the country, probably at Hetzen-dorf.   We are told that it arose out of a (transient) happy love affair, but nothing further is known about it, unless the source of inspiration is to be found in the relations with Giulietta, though it is not love exactly that breathes from this music.   It seems rather, as remarked before, as though its writer had sought refuge from far too agitating emotions in the peace of Nature.

The love of Nature was a prominent feature in the character of this genius.   He never undertook long journeys, he did not succeed in reaching grand scenery like that of Switzerland or the Tyrol ; a visit to Italy remained one of his unfulfilled dreams.   But at the first sign of spring he set out from Vienna, eager to give up town life for that of the idyllic villages amongst the forest-clad hills in the " Wienerwald."   As a rule he would stay there as far into the autumn as possible, only now and then paying a flying visit to Vienna.   Sometimes, when he went

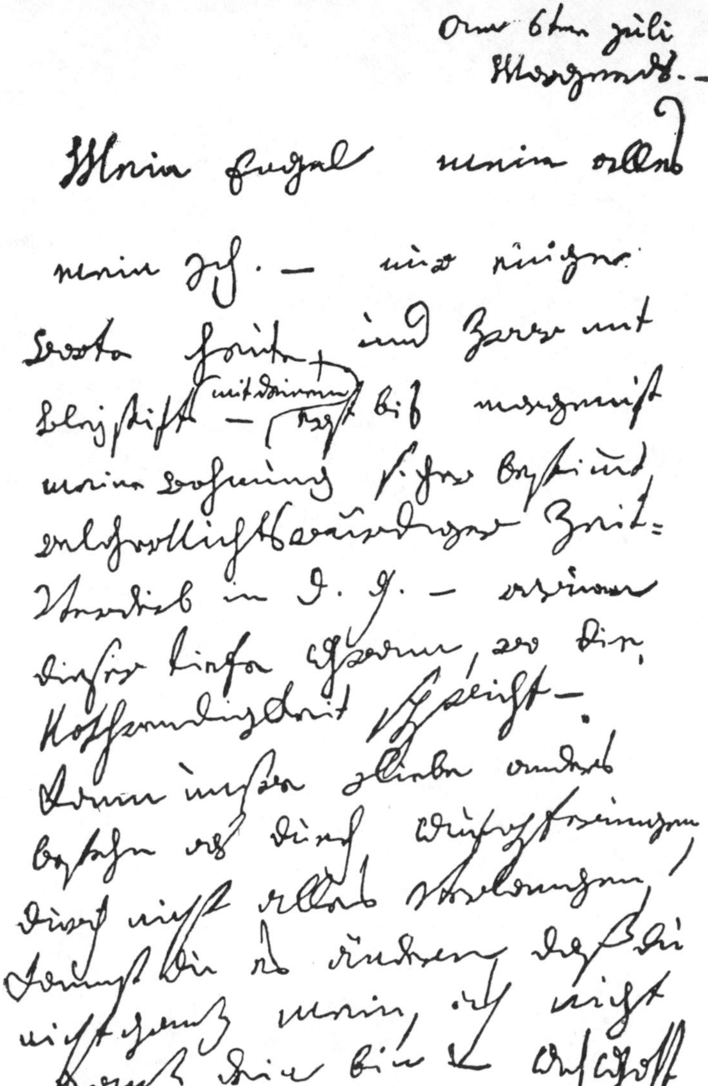
am 6ten Juli
Morgends. —

Mein Engel, mein alles, mein Ich. — nur einige Worte heute, und zwar mit Bleystift (mit deinem) — erst bis morgen ist meine Wohnung sicher bestimmt, welcher nichtswürdiger Zeitverderb in d. g. — warum dieser tiefe Gram, wo die Nothwendigkeit spricht — kann unsre Liebe anders bestehn als durch Aufopferungen, durch nicht alles verlangen, kannst du es ändern, daß du nicht ganz mein, ich nicht ganz dein bin — Ach Gott

First Page of the Letter to "the immortally Beloved."

further afield on these summer journeys, it would be either to visit his wealthy and aristocratic friends at their country houses (as in Hungary and Silesia), or to seek relief for now one, now another physical ailment at famous watering-places, such as Carlsbad or Teplitz. " No one can love the country as I do —forests, trees, rocks, they give the response that one desires " ; and, one might add, that Beethoven often looked for in vain amongst human beings. His love for the country was therefore all the greater, and its peace and solitude the deepest solace to his spirit. It was a relief to him, too, because of his failing sense of hearing. " My miserable hearing does not worry me here. It is as though every tree spoke to me in the country. Holy, holy ! To be in the woods is ecstasy. Who can describe it—the sweet stillness of the woods ! "

Nature was indeed holy to him, as a sheer image of the divine. His mind was full of pantheistic ideas, and they were a part of his contemplation of Nature. " Almighty !—in the forest—I am blissfully happy in the forest, every tree speaks to me of Thee, O God ! How glorious—amongst these woods— on these heights there is peace—peace to serve Him ! " One can imagine from these impulsive, hymn-like ejaculations what it was that occupied his mind and imagination. And, con- scious of the significant part that Nature played in his creative power, he once writes, of the pleasant fir-woods at Baaden (near Vienna) : " There Beethoven often created poems, or, as it is said, composed them." It is characteristic of Beethoven that he calls these musical ideas with which Nature has inspired him " poems." He felt, as it were, that the roots of his art went down to the primeval cause of things ; Nature, eternal and free, was a deep and frequent source of inspiration to him. The octogenarian English pianist, Neate, who in his youth saw a great deal of Beethoven, declared to Thayer that he had never met anyone who loved Nature as Beethoven did. This was evidently one of Neate's strongest impressions of the

G

Master's natural disposition; he says of it, " Nature was, as it were, his nourishment; he seemed actually to live on her."

The Nature mood of the sonata is of an idyllic kind. On a larger scale, and in more varied manner, but hardly a more poetical one, Beethoven's Nature-joy and worship found utterance later in the " Pastoral Symphony," with its dread of storm and its closing hymn. The pastoral element in the sonata arises from the numerous resting pedal points, the calmly contemplative musical expression, the undulating time beats (3/4, 6/8), the long, gently sung melodies. The first in the *Allegro*, with its genuinely pastoral, bugle-like closing section, which forms an important part in the modulation, might, from its simplicity and peculiar rhythmic displacement, be taken as a prototype of a page from the music of Brahms. The very choice of tonality, which, as we have seen, was an important point with Beethoven, contributes to the pastoral mood. D major ranks equally with E major in being thus understood.

And yet, Beethoven could not write an insipid Sundayish idyll. There is a certain penetrating power even in the calm movements and their leading subjects, and the Sonata exhibits effective, powerful contrasts, not only those mentioned above, in the *Andante*, but also in the short, almost frolicking *Scherzo*. It seems to be a forerunner of the merry gathering of country folk, " Lustiges Zusammensein der Landleute "—the ascending of the single thirds through the sixths to the whole of the closely placed triad, giving the impression of more and more merry " country folk," crowding up and taking part in the fun. The pastoral character of the *Finale* is asserted at once by the solo *basso ostinato* at the beginning, and later by the quiet emotion controlling the movement. This movement too, with its broad outlines and its sedate *tempo* (" Allegro ma non troppo "), may be considered a forerunner of the *Finale* in the " Pastoral Symphony " with its " Thanksgiving Song." Riemann's searching analysis has shown that it is connected by many delicate threads with the earlier work, especially the first *Allegro* of the sonata.

Regarded as a whole the sonata is a simple and unreflecting tribute to the beauty and peace of Nature and rural surroundings. To endow it with mystery or reproduce Nature in fantastic and mysterious imagery, as the composers of the romantic school did not long after, was not Beethoven's way. Even Franz Schubert, who came soon after, looked at Nature and listened to her in a different way from Ludwig van Beethoven.

CHAPTER IX

EVEN the exterior circumstances connected with Beethoven's Opus 31 are peculiar. For various reasons three piano sonatas were included in one "work," which now stands as a milestone in the series, in so far as two of the sonatas, each in its own way, point onward in the Master's production, while the third looks back to a stage which he has almost left behind him.

Opus 31 comprises the sonatas in G major, D minor and E flat major, but they were not originally intended to appear as a musical trefoil. They did not constitute a unity in Beethoven's mind, and it is chiefly from a historical point of view that their mutual contrasts become interesting. The origin of this Opus is also responsible for the absence of any dedication, although the first of the three seems to have been intended for a lady admirer, who had given occasion to its being composed, and had been given the prospect of a dedication. But the plan was not carried out, and as the sonata in its ultimate form was grouped with two others, the name of this lady has never become known.* It was " the lady's " idea that Beethoven

* The lady in question may have been the Countess Browne to whom Opus 10 is dedicated. According to Lenz it is said that there is even another edition (in Russia ?) of the sonata, with a French title and bearing a dedication to the Countess. Yet the matter seems to be doubtful. That the request came from a Leipzig publisher and that Beethoven in his answer, apparently in ignorance, only mentions " the lady," does not, at any rate, recall the Vienna beauty to one's mind. Wilibald Nagel has found a letter from a Countess Kielmannsegg (who, according to rumour, by the way, was the mistress of Napoleon and the mother of one of his sons), the contents of which might indicate that *she* was the unknown client who had given the " commission " for the sonata, but who, on account of the Master's exaggerated claims (as regards fee ?) again withdrew from the affair. Nagel admits, though, that he is unable to produce any evidence to prove his conjecture. Possibly it is quite permissible to agree with his opinion that Beethoven was inspired after all by the peculiar " commission " to write the sonata.

should write—a " Revolution Sonata " !   When the young
Master learned that this was the object of the commission he
gave his indignation and sarcasm a free rein in his letter to the
publisher, Hoffmeister of Leipzig.   The letter, abrupt in form
and not exactly courteous in tone, is very characteristic of him :
" Are you crazy, gentlemen ! To propose that I should write
a sonata of *that* sort !   During the fever of the Revolution,
well, yes, let that pass, but now, when people are simmering
down ; Bonaparte has concluded a Concordat with the Pope
—such a sonata, now ?—Heàvens above ! in these new Christian times, humph !—No, leave me alone, I shall do nothing of
the kind."

The G major sonata then, the ultimate outcome of these
ill-advised proposals, certainly does not bear the slightest trace
of revolution.   On the contrary, it is serene, bright and gay.
It might be called the staccato sonata, as the staccatos
predominate in a marked degree over the legatos in both
the first and second movements.   This gives the music
a piquant, and now and then a playful character ; so
playful, in fact, that one might be tempted to consider the
sonata a musical-ironical protest against the revolutionary
idea that was to have been forced upon Beethoven.   An
example in point is the *Adagio*, which is labelled " grazioso "—
surely a unique term for such a movement.   Moreover, it is
exactly in that slightly old-fashioned style, ornamental and
circumstantial, that must have reminded listeners of the good
old times ; besides, the resemblance to a C major Aria in
The Creation (of Haydn) is striking and *perhaps* not accidental.
Yet Beethoven does not disown his ideas in this movement ;
we recognise his tonĕ, where he passes over in the " knocking "
bass from C minor to the broad and beautiful A flat major
melody so characteristic of him.   It is true that he soon returns
to the original mode : the old-fashioned daintiness is again
uppermost and the graceful ornamentation becomes even richer

and more prominent. The bass figures and the employment of thirds (and sixths) may also have reminded the audience of a favourite Italian manner in use earlier. The sonata has no *Scherzo ;* with his growing sense of unity and character Beethoven would feel that in this instance, in which brightness and gaiety, playfulness and humour prevail throughout, there is really no need of a *Scherzo* piece. In the Rondo *Finale* we again encounter the pleasantly jovial indoor tone, with touches of genuine Beethoven humour.

This G major sonata, with the marked rhythmic character of the first movement, owes its origin, by the way, to an outline for a string quartet that was never completed. Beethoven now intended it for the publisher and composer Nägeli of Zürich, but his brother Carl wanted him to sell it to a Leipzig publisher, no doubt with a view to obtaining a higher price. Carl and the second brother, Johan, often interfered in a tactless and selfish manner in the publishing affairs of their celebrated but unpractical brother, who had neither the heart nor the courage to tell them to mind their own business. During a walk at Heiligenstadt the two brothers (Ludwig and Carl), who were both quick-tempered, grew so excited in discussing this matter that it is said they came to blows. The story is not improbable ; Carl, at any rate, being so hot-tempered and so lacking in self-control that he once stabbed his wife in the hand with a table-knife in a domestic quarrel !

Beethoven had his way in the choice of a publisher, however, and when the matter was settled he sought reconciliation with his brother in the most generous way, as he had so often done before. But he gained no satisfaction from going to Nägeli. The worthy man took upon himself to make corrections in the work that had been entrusted to him for publication—after all, he was a bit of a composer too ! In his opinion the first movement would gain by the addition of four bars, and these he therefore composed himself. When reading the proof-sheets,

Beethoven of course discovered this audacity and was furious.
" Where the devil is that written ? " he shouted, and it is said
that " his surprise and anger were indescribable." The four
bars were struck out at once, all other faults corrected, and the
sonata was sent to Simrock in Bonn with emphatic instructions
to publish it as *Édition très correcte.*

The G major sonata, then, together with the D minor that
followed it, appeared in 1803 at Simrock's ; but the Opus 31,
as we know it, comprising all the three sonatas mentioned
above, did not appear till 1805 in a Vienna edition, and then
bore the Opus number 29.   This is an example of the confusion
that may sometimes be found in the numbering of Beethoven's
works.   Meanwhile the Master's wrath did not deter the
enterprising Zürich publisher from printing the sonata (1803)
in his *Répertoire des Clavicinistes.*

However, it is not this G major sonata that sets its stamp
upon Opus 31.   To use Beethoven's own expression about an
earlier sonata, it cannot, at any rate, be classed among the
" corkers,"—the important link in the Opus is formed by the
next sonata in D minor.

The sonata has a fantasia character resembling that of the
two *quasi fantasia* sonatas of Opus 27 ; but it is less intimate
than either of these.   There are lines of pain about its
physiognomy—as there generally are in Beethoven's music when
he chooses this key—but they do not hide themselves from the
beholder.   Suffering, the agitated mind, the interior struggle
of the soul, are openly and strongly expressed, as though
imploring sympathy and understanding.   In other words, the
sonata is not purely typical, rather it is dramatic in character,
and so far it is a forerunner of the " Appassionata."   This it is,
furthermore, because the Master has been successful in creating a tragic subject according to the principle: unity within the
cyclical form.   Though the subject in the F minor sonata is
more stupendous, the mastery with which it is handled more

imposing, and the artistic whole consequently firmer and closer than in the present case, this does not conceal the resemblance. It even extends to details, such as the way in which the first stormy *Allegros* sink into a dull murmur, in a long-sustained clinging to the leading minor tonality, without really attaining to rest or calmness at the close.

The surging and ominous *Arpeggios* at the beginning of this first *Allegro*, the disquieting quaver-figures, the themes rising from the depths and breaking in the shrill tones of the treble, the broken chords in concert style and the sudden speaking recitatives (which really do utter a man's speech and ought to be played as such, and, as it has justly been pointed out, like the recitatives in the ninth symphony : " selon le caractère d'un récitatif, mais in tempo ")—all these qualities make the movement a remarkable piece in Beethoven's music from this first part of his manhood. If one looks for the deeper relation between the Master's work and the events of his life, one will involuntarily find the text of this tone poem in the well-known " Heiligenstadt Testament." Is it not as though one heard in the manly defiance and plaint of the recitatives the opening words of this human document : " Oh, ye human beings, who think I am hostile, crazy or misanthropical, how you wrong me. . . ." ?

This conception is strengthened when we know that the sonata was written at exactly the same time as the " Testament," and that the first movement, unlike so much of Beethoven's other music, was created " straight off." The sketch-book shows that it stood complete in Beethoven's mind in all its main outlines. Perhaps he even wrote it down in a few hours, possibly while wandering in the country where the " Testament " was also written. An imperative need to tell " human beings " of his sufferings, of the struggle and conflict in his soul, then finds utterance both in sounds and in actual words. And, as Goethe says, a god gave him the power to express what he suffered. To such a height as this had he attained in human and artistic development.

If this be a correct explanation of the origin and prevailing mood of the sonata, one need not go so far as Shakespeare's *Tempest* in seeking to understand it (or the sonata Opus 57 in affinity with it). A. Schindler has related that, in answer to his question about the key to the two works, Beethoven answered curtly, " Read Shakespeare's *Tempest !* " Schindler was a devoted admirer of Beethoven, and a great help to him in his later years, when his health was failing and he was harassed by many cares, but, intellectually speaking, Beethoven was head and shoulders above him ; Schindler had not even the stature of an Eckermann beside his Goethe. May not this answer, then, have been meant merely as a biting or a jesting and mocking evasion ? It does not seem to have any artistic value. It is difficult, in fact, to find the relation between this very dramatic first movement and the festival play which is perhaps the least dramatic of Shakespeare's works. In the *Finale* of the sonata one might suspect a glimpse of the English Master's imaginary world and of a sad and gentle Ariel's fare-well flight. But what has become of Caliban's uncouth tumbling about, and why translate the symbolism of the *Tempest* into the world of sound at all ? Nevertheless it is well known that Beethoven had the greatest admiration for Shakespeare's genius, and that he had entered deeply into the spirit of its inspired frenzy, and of the creatures of light and darkness born of it. The reading of Shakespeare's dramas was an essential part of Beethoven's mental nourishment and may possibly often have inspired him in his work. His answer may therefore be inter-preted in a general sense, without being applied to this par-ticular sonata in connection with the *Tempest*.

Beethoven, in fact, neither aimed at nor wished to write what is called nowadays illustrative or " programme " music. He was too great for that, too free, too independent an artist. But it is quite certain that he created many of his works from the germ of a poetical idea—as one might perhaps call it—which he desired to endow with life in this way and put before his audience. This subject cannot be further developed here, but, to elucidate the Master's conception of this artistic point, the following is worth mentioning: A Beethoven society had been formed at Bremen under the leadership of Dr. W. C. Müller and his daughter Elise, and when the Master heard of this he was so pleased that he once said, " he wished he had Oberon's horn that he might be transported thither." Now a minor poet there, Dr. von Iken, had undertaken to write appropriate verses to Beethoven's various works, including the sonatas. Specimens were sent to the Master, with a request for his approval of this poetic interpretation, but he rejected the proposal in a friendly spirit : " His music did not require a programme or a detailed verbal interpretation ; should there, after all, be any need of explanations at concert recitals, he desired them to restrict themselves to a general survey of the character of the compositions " ; which really means the same as their " poetic idea " mentioned above.

In the main the dramatic element is concluded with the first *Allegro* of the sonata, yet, as indicated before, without any deliverance being reached at the close. This sonata has already been termed a forerunner of the " Appassionata," and, as in the latter, the first *Allegro* is followed by a quiet movement, its calmness being the outcome of the previous struggle, and its lighter air holding out hopes of a less troubled existence, yet not in this work either does Beethoven rise to any *Scherzo* mood. In the *Finale* we return to the sombre *D minor* key ; there is a yearning and straining as in the first movement, but as though transported into another world, in a strangely light and delicate atmosphere—the whole has the effect of an impalpable dream. One may perhaps think of a fantastic nightmare ; the link is then formed with the tradition which naïvely tells us that Beethoven was indebted for this rhythm to the hoof-beats of a galloping horse! It certainly cannot be an ordinary earthly equine creature that rushes through this piece of music. It may be classed, by the way, amongst those that one would fain wish to be spared the madly rapid *tempo* of a virtuoso, which may easily give it a slovenly and study-like air.

We have been told that the D minor sonata is amongst those which Beethoven himself valued highly and which he played by preference in public. This is easily understood, partly because of the concert style possessed in a certain degree by this sonata, partly because, in the marked outlines and concentration of this work, he could interpret his deep emotions in a vivid tone-language.

In the third sonata, still included in this Opus 31, he speaks in another tongue. This sonata is written in E flat major, and it is a characteristic feature that the composer only finds his way to this key through a sort of questioning theme and a series of bars in no definite tonality. D minor and E flat major! These two favourite keys of Beethoven's, so fundamentally different in character, here following closely after each other— it seems once again an instance of the phenomenon peculiar to Beethoven, that after having sung out his lament, and found deliverance from his deep despondency through his art, he turns to the opposite of these moods, here to E flat, that is, his heroic key and that in which he expresses his manly joy, his healthy optimism.

Yet (in this E flat sonata) he does not rise to any actually heroic mood. The sonata is slighter in style, but its language is forceful and strong, spiced with a bold humour sustained by the Master's delightful and charming confidence and clearness. The sonata—as the contrast to the D minor—is all confiding harmony; anxiety and dread are almost entirely thrown aside; it seems to have been done lightly and with a master hand; if such moods do appear momentarily they are speedily put to flight.

Unhappily we know nothing definite about the possible

exterior or interior causes of its creation. Thus, nothing is known of any sketches for the sonata, but it was written at about the same time as the two others. Notwithstanding its beauty it is put in the shade somewhat (as regards public recitals) by those most nearly related to it in the series and written more in concert style, the D minor, C major and F minor sonatas. To Hugo Riemann the subject of the sonata represents the eagle flight of genius set free from its earthly coil. Yet it would seem that it might be interpreted simply as a natural reaction after the gloom of the D minor in the previous sonata, and this would quite agree with Beethoven's usual method of working, assuming that he worked at both sonatas at the same time. In the present instance it is all the more probable, as this music contains a sort of determination, suggestive of a deliberate will to cope with life, an energetic effort to rise above all that is heavy and oppressive. But, as said before, there are no grand heroics here, the subject of this sonata is not a matter of life and death, and therefore does not evoke many impressions of an eagle's flight against the sun. Most people would scent in it a wholesome fragrance of the soil. The soundness and force of this sonata come from its rhythmic buoyancy and the ingenious application of rhythmic effects, and henceforward Beethoven's interest and inventive impulse are more and more attracted to this means of effect. The tone language of this sonata is as far from grand speeches as from external brilliance ; on the contrary, it is peculiarly downright in its tone, almost confidential, with flashes of gay humour ; it is harmonically clear and controlled—until the *Finale*, when it seems that the artist is so overwhelmed by vitality that his manly talk, hitherto firm, breaks into jubilant, irrepressible, youthful frolics.

The sonata has no slow movement ; there is no room here for visions, laments or feelings ! In a *Scherzo*, the first *great* one in the sonatas, fairly bursting with strength and sparkling rhythm, and more worked out than any middle movement hitherto, Beethoven employs a new mode of effect, which, as stated earlier, he gained for the piano, and which we shall see him using more and more : the staccato. The freedom and newness of this movement are already indicated in the time signature, the triple time traditional in this section being abandoned. The whole movement is a masterpiece of technique, invention and humour. A *Menuetto*, not unintentionally called *grazioso*, seems to recall memories of a youthful cult of Haydn and Mozart ; the Minuet otherwise disappearing gradually from Beethoven's sonata-works. Here he has brought it out, however, and once more we meet with its graceful dignity, stamped by his personal interpretation. It is as though one saw and heard the rustle of silken trains over brightly polished parquet floors, and perceived dignified, gently playful glances and courtly compliments. The Trio, on the other hand, points to the future, as far ahead even as Schumann ; and a modern master of technique, Camille Saint-Saëns, has, in fact, employed these bars as a subject for a series of brilliant variations for two pianos. In the very singular Coda Beethoven seems to withdraw from the elegant diversion, to turn his back on the ballroom and with a wistful sigh leave the dancers—his kingdom is no longer of this world.

What his true kingdom is, the *Finale* already reveals to us in a momentary gleam. It races on through storm and gale, defiant and gay in its valiant assurance of its own force and strength. Hence the intrepid display, in a rushing torrent of all the pianistic mastery he now possessed, and which he caused to gleam and sparkle, not for its own sake, but as the means of freely expressing deeply personal and sublime ideas. One may therefore agree with Hugo Riemann in considering this sonata, and especially its *Finale*, as the last preparation for those gigantic piano-works, the " Waldstein " and the " Appassionata " sonatas. On the other hand, it is perhaps more difficult to understand how the same writer can hear " the trembling of the universe " and "Wotan sweeping across the seas and over mountain forests," even when understanding which rhythmic passages he imagined to be the riding of Wotan. On the other hand, it is quite impossible to understand that another writer could be content to interpret the *Finale* as—a tarantella ! This movement has as little to do with dance music, however ennobled and enlarged in form, as with the riding of Wotan. This glorious and sovereign tone-drama of Beethoven's does not, in fact, need either one or the other of such " explanations."

Beethoven's Opus 31 is a remarkable triad amongst his piano works—arising as it did arbitrarily, or almost accidentally, and yet having its own features and peculiar significance in the series of the sonatas. It shows within small limits the wealth of genius in its varying moods and forms of expression, sometimes directly opposed to each other, in the first section pointing back to the youthful, essentially artistic stage, and in the two others forward, and that again in different ways, partly to a greater and greater pianistic perfection of many facets, partly to a more dramatic style. At the time when these sonatas were written, Beethoven is said to have stated that he was not satisfied with his earlier works. " Henceforth I will walk in a new path," he added. He may have alluded to a great work like the " Eroica " Symphony, which was perhaps then already forming in his mind ; but the Opus 31 D minor and E flat major sonatas can also testify to his determination to find new paths. A friend, who felt that there was something new and surprising in them, on asking whether a particular place in the D minor sonata " was good," received from Beethoven the characteristic answer, " Yes, of course it's good ! But you are of the same country as *Krumpholz*—you cannot get that kind of thing into your thick Bohemian head ! "

*   *   *   *   *   *

Beethoven is now ready and ripe for the two great sonatas, the " Waldstein " and the " Appassionata," but they are preceded in the series by two " Sonates faciles " (in G minor and

G major), Opus 49. They are really sonatinas, each in only two movements; the first consisting of an *Andante* and an *Allegro*, the second of an *Allegro* and a *Menuetto*. These two simple musical works, in which there is hardly any working out of the theme, are not, as was at one time supposed, early attempts at compositions by Beethoven when quite young, which now found favour on closer examination. Yet their origin undoubtedly dates back some years—compared with the last-mentioned Opus, again a proof of how unreliable Beethoven's Opus numbers are in a chronological respect.

The sonata in G major dates from 1796. It is therefore strange, puzzling, in fact, how Hugo Riemann can find that it is a contrast in mood to the subject and tone of the " Heiligenstadt Testament." The two things seem to have nothing to do with each other, psychologically, and as Beethoven did not write the " Testament " till 1802, this excludes any connection between them. The sonata in D minor dates from the year 1798. According to Shedlock there are some sketch-books in the British Museum containing sketch upon sketch, drafts worked out over and over again for these small sonatas, which were probably written for the use of Beethoven's pupils. At that time he still gave some guidance in piano playing to ladies of rank and others. The absence of any dedication on this Opus also indicates that they were originally meant for purposes of study. In this capacity the two sonatas probably circulated in manuscript or in copies, until they were printed in 1805, at the instance, it seems, of the business-like brother Carl. Whether it is due to him or another publisher equally capable that the sonatas were advertised with doubtful accuracy, as " quite new," is a matter on which we have no certain information.

The Minuet in D major has a motif, which in its main outlines was employed in Beethoven's Septette, the latter dating from the year 1800.

CHAPTER X

THE sonata in C major, Opus 53, is believed to have been composed in 1803–4. It was published in 1805 under the title of " Grande Sonate," the right name indeed for this work, which possesses more grandeur than any previous sonata, and the stamp of a work written on concert scale. It has also, more than any of them, won for itself a place in concert-rooms.

The sonata was dedicated to Count Ferdinand von Waldstein, and one may venture to believe that this dedication was a matter nearer to Beethoven's heart than many of the others. In the early days in Bonn, Count Waldstein, with his alert, enlightened mind and his understanding love of art, was amongst the first to perceive the genius of the Court singer's son. It was to him, as we have already seen, that Beethoven to a great extent owed the connection with Haydn and the aristocratic world of Vienna.

At Bonn, Count Waldstein, who was eight years older than Beethoven, presented the latter with a grand piano for his training as a pianist. He also assisted him financially, having the delicacy and tact to let the young musician think that the money was an acknowledgment of musical services rendered to the Elector. It is very probable that the " Ritterballet " which Beethoven composed at Bonn was a token of his appreciation of the young Count, when the latter was raised to the knighthood of a German order in 1788. (The music appeared anonymously in 1791, and Count Waldstein does not seem to have contradicted those who assumed it to be *his* work !) The lines on an album leaf, written on the occasion of the composer's departure for Vienna and quoted in every biography of

Beethoven, will always remain a link between the two names. No letters seem to have been preserved from any correspondence between the two men—or musicians, one might say, as Count Waldstein was more than an amateur at music, but there is no reason to suppose that the good relations between them were ever interrupted or clouded over, as we know that they were unhappily in the case of several other friends of Beethoven. They remained unbroken for a long time, in any case ; for a remark in the " conversation-books " might be taken to indicate that an estrangement or coolness did ultimately supervene.

As a fervent patriot Count Waldstein later separated from the Elector at Bonn, with whom he had been particularly intimate, as the latter seemed to have engaged in a political coquetry with France, and the Count then obtained Austrian permission to offer his services to England. His last years were spent in Vienna, where he died childless at the age of sixty-one, four years before Beethoven. He seems to have been a man of more than usual worth, and of sterling character, besides being both a cultivated and extremely charming personality, the type of a refined and aristocratic Viennese of that time. A contemporary has thus described him : " He is very intellectual and culti- vated, and his knowledge is extensive. He is a man who can appreciate a good table, and has a refined taste in wine. He is an admirable musician and improvises delightfully on the piano. He is a reliable and devoted friend ; he has humour and he is charitable in his opinion of others. In regard to politics it is impossible to be of a better spirit than he. He is as dear to me as a brother. A finer and more genuine character than his cannot be imagined."

One can understand that Beethoven would feel attached to such a man, who was worthy of his friendship and had filled a large place in the early years of his life. His craving for the affection and sympathy of his fellow-men seems to have been satisfied in an unusual degree in this instance.

H

We may therefore believe that the dedication of the C major sonata " came from the heart " and " went to the heart " (as Beethoven wrote on his *Missa solemnis*). But besides these human, fraternal feelings for Count Waldstein, memories were linked with this name. Memories of childhood's days and the life in Bonn, though not very happy ones—far from it. Yet Beethoven never forgot his birthplace and the country around it ; right up to his latest years he clung to it, and no doubt the passage of time softened in his remembrance much that was bitter and dark, and the town on the Rhine remained, grown beautiful in the soft radiance shed on it by the memories of childhood. It is not strange that in the first letters from Vienna he dwells on his life in Bonn, writing in 1801 to Wegeler : " My fatherland is still as clear and beautiful to my mind's eye as when I left you " ; and at about the same time to his friend Amenda : " You are no *Vienna-friend*, no, you are of the kind that the soil of my country produces." There is also the touching story from 1812 about the young gardener who brought Beethoven letters from his father, the director of the public gardens in Bonn, and from Ferdinand Ries. Beethoven was deeply moved on hearing his Bonn dialect and received him very cordially. " I can understand *you*," exclaimed the great Master, " you speak ' Bönnisch ' " (the Bonn dialect). " You must be my guest on Sunday at ' The White Swan ! ' " As late as 1823 Beethoven writes to Ries, who was then living in Bonn : " Farewell, thou ever-dear Rhine country." In the letter quoted in an earlier chapter, of 1826, from Beethoven to Wegeler, in which he says that he still has a silhouette of Eleonore von Breuning, he adds, " You can see from this how I treasure everything from my youth that is dear and good."

Even without any direct evidence about it there is reason to believe that both the memories of the country round his home and his affection for the friend of his youth have had their share in the composition of the " poem," as Beethoven

himself calls it, of the C major sonata. Moreover, a direct
proof has been found in the song melody in the last movement,
which is said to have come from a Rhineland folk-song. It
belongs, by the way, to those melodies peculiar to Beethoven,
arising in the music, charming in their beauty, but not brought
to a formal conclusion, though the lack of this is not felt. We
have met with this type of melody before and we shall meet
it again; for instance, in the F sharp major, Opus 78, 1st
movement; E major, Opus 90, 2nd movement; A flat major,
Opus 110, 1st movement; C minor, Opus 111, 1st movement.
It also occurs, of course, in Beethoven's other works, such as
in the " Coriolan " Overture, in the F minor quartette and
others.

*   *   *   *   *   *

We can imagine, then, how Beethoven's mind was stirred
when he wrote this sunshine sonata. At any rate no one can
have any doubt about the light-hearted happiness that finds
expression in this music. At the very beginning of the sonata
one may perhaps find a symbol of it in the contrast between
the monotonous murmur in the deeper tones of the instrument and the little, darting *motif* in its upper notes, which
develops into an exultant series of semiquavers. This little
motif, characteristic of Beethoven's style at this time, is not
really a melody, but a rhythmic motion; it attains to promin-
ence in the movement and is countered by the beautiful hymn-
like E-major *motif*, which is a more direct expression of deliverance leading to interior harmony. The way in which the
latter appears, first in calm, broad harmonies, then spun into
triplet figurations, might remind one of the piano concertos
with the interplay of piano and orchestra. Meanwhile this is
not any piece of musical conflict, such as we find so often in
Beethoven's instrumental works of this (so-called " second ")
period. The deliverance, the happiness, seems to be present
from the beginning, it is not attained through strife and sharp

contrasts; altogether there are but few minor chords in this sonata, the subject of which expresses more and more clearly the light and splendour radiating from a harmonious soul attuned to joy. The close of the movement is very poetic : into the radiant and majestic stream of sound the hymn-like motif ventures to whisper, *piano dolce*, like a memory, pleading, warning; but in his ecstatic joy the composer does not listen to its speech, its lingering notes are broken swiftly and resolutely, so that the rhythmic motif which has prevailed in the movement gets the last word, followed by a few *ff* chords. This mood in the first movement now yields for a few moments to the beautiful introduction to the Rondo finale, and more plaintive moods find expression in the *Molto Adagio* tempo. The mind seems stirred by a strange wave-like motion; unlike the firmness of the first *Allegro*, the *Adagio* finds only transient rest in the melody it utters, but as it is swayed more and more by the waves it emerges again, this time in that very melody of the Rhineland which may have sprung from the memories of childhood that have inspired this sonata, or that have been awakened while the composer was at work on it. In a *tempo* which Beethoven, by adding the word *moderato*, expressly wishes to guard from being hurried, this melody gracefully unfolds itself from the introduction, gliding out like sunshine and diaphanous mists over the ever-dear Rhine, the rippling of whose waves it does not need much imagination to hear in the figuration woven round the melody. The whole piece is bathed in beautiful, undimmed sunshine, notwithstanding the incidental minor melodies; they seem only to give the movement a peculiar boldness. In its rich colouring it suggests a taste of ripe grapes !

In compass the largest *Finale* that Beethoven had yet given to any sonata, it shows, in its brilliant concert style, like the rest of the sonata, the Master's intimacy with his instrument and his clear and unerring handling of it. A mastery like this was

57334

able to evoke this stream of poetry from the instrument.   The
" Sonata of the Dawn " is the not ill-chosen name once given
to this sonata !

To us this work now seems to be of such firm and organic
construction that it is difficult to believe the account of Ferdinand Ries, who says that in its original form it had a large independent middle movement, the *Andante* in F major, which was
taken out later and published independently under the name
of *Andante favori*.   A friend of Beethoven—can it have been
Ries himself ?—is said to have remarked to him that with this
comprehensive *Andante* the Sonata would attain to an unwieldy
size and be far too long, in the opinion of those days.   Even
though the hot-headed Master disagreed emphatically with
this, he took occasion later to act upon the suggestion.   The
Andante was taken out and replaced by the present *Introduzione*.   Owing to the perfect form that the sonata now seems
to possess, this account has not always been believed ; but it
has gained in credibility by Thayer's remark (in a catalogue of
Beethoven's works), that in the MS. *Introduzione* is written
with quite another kind of ink than the rest of the sonata,
and has therefore evidently been inserted later.

Nor is it easy to believe that the length of the sonata would
be a deciding factor in making Beethoven eliminate the F major
Andante, but he may well have been constrained to do so for
artistic reasons.   He may have felt that a contrasting section
or a transition of a more serious and introspective character
was needed between the two impetuous and brilliant outer
movements.   With the *Andante* the sonata as a whole would
have been too monochrome, and the brilliant concert style,
which in the F major *Andante* becomes almost ingratiating
and intimate, would dominate the sonata more than fitting in
a chamber music work.

Meanwhile, as it is, the sonata is resplendent with virtuoso
features, with glittering runs and passages, though they are not

an aim in themselves, like those here and there in the earlier works, but issue from the intention to clothe the bright, radiant music as expressively and effectively as possible. The sonata has cadenza parts and rapid triplet passages, it has a wealth of tremolos, in the Rondo especially, it has whole chains of trills ringing out their joy through several bars, and joined to the leading melody in a new and effective manner. Beethoven himself writes about these trills, that if the passage is found to be too difficult, it can be made easier by various alterations, which he indicates himself, observing in conclusion that it is not a matter of great importance even if this long trill loses something of its usual value; a remark showing that Beethoven was well aware that he had written for a practised concert pianist rather than for the private devotee of the art of piano playing.

It is probable that the idea for the sonata arose in Beethoven's mind in the beginning of the year in which he played in public his C minor concerto, a stupendous achievement in those days, regarded both as a composition and from the point of view of technique. May one not suppose, then, that his joyous sense of victory, in having been able to show his audience what he could make his instrument produce, would still be tingling in him when he completed the sonata? It has the interplay between concert music and intimate sonata to which we alluded before. The radiance of the C major sonata can hardly come only from the reflections of memories of childhood, but must be due also to the composer's joy in the consciousness of the mastery he now possessed.

*   *   *   *   *   *

Meanwhile the Waldstein sonata represents in the series only a temporary deliverance from gloom and despondency. If we did not know from other sources, from letters and the accounts of contemporaries, as well as from such works as the C minor symphony, what was still oppressing Beethoven, and what he had to struggle against within and without, we should have a presentiment of it in the great looming shadow of the " Appassionata," which is now drawing close upon us.

It is preceded by only one sonata work, the small F major sonata, Opus 54, in two movements. Very little is known of the origin of this work, which, not without reason, has no distinguished place in the series, and has never been popular, hardly more than slightly known, either by the public or by pianists, to whom it offers difficult but rather thankless tasks. It carries no dedication, and judging from the sketch-books it does not seem to have filled Beethoven's mind or thoughts as much as similar works often did : the first disconnected outlines are found in the sketch-books immediately before the sonata in its final form, and, as though symbolically, at the same time as the outlines for the work that was to cause him so much distress, " Fidelio," and for one of his least popular and least inspired concert works, the so-called " Triple Concerto, Opus 56."

It may perhaps be supposed that the sonata served purposes of teaching; in any case it shows Beethoven's preoccupation with technical problems, but while the E flat (Opus 31) and C major (Opus 53) sonatas show the victory of musical ideas over technique, the technical here seems to be uppermost, so that the subject is somewhat put in the shade. Nohl already called the sonata "a study," though he carefully added, " but certainly a Master's study."

The first movement, bearing the remarkable term, " In tempo d'un menuetto," can hardly be considered a study. It is a piece full of character, slightly rugged and inaccessible, in which two diverse subjects are set one against the other, in direct and unmediated opposition without ever attaining to any fusion, such as Beethoven might and could have brought about, had he wished to do so. That he did not, must therefore have been from a certain intention which cannot now be traced. Towards the end the composer remodels the first hard or rather robust theme, so that it becomes gentler and almost visionary. It has been suggested that in this form it has a resemblance to a Swedish folk-song. This may be accidental, though in his later years, and perhaps even at this time, Beethoven became interested in studying the folk-songs of various countries. It is, therefore, quite possible that there is a re-echo of a folk-song in this piano work, though we do not know whether a definite Swedish melody was known to the Master or present in his mind. As we know, the study of folk-songs bore other fruits in his production. Another reminder of them may perhaps be pointed out in a later sonata (Opus 101).

The running semi-quaver figures of the *Finale* already show an external relationship with the *Finale* of the sonata in A flat major, Opus 26. It cannot be denied that this sonata, too, has somewhat the character of a study, and is not particularly inspired or communicative. But the movement, with its clear and, as it were, objective stream of music, in a style which seems to foretell the " last " sonatas, and with its elaborate detail, is still a piece of music which bears the imprint of genius, especially from a harmonic (modulatory) and rhythmic point of view. Though unappreciated by several writers, this *Finale* too contains the germs of future music. The effect produced by this sonata in its own day can be seen in a criticism in the *Leipzig Musical Times*, in which it is said to be " difficult to play," " written in an eccentric spirit," but " full of extraordinary whims."

CHAPTER XI

WHEN did Beethoven write his Opus 57, the Sonata in F minor, perhaps the most famous of them all and the most frequently played, and still known as the "Appassionata," although the Master himself never gave it that name?

It cannot be stated with certainty when the sonata was composed. Schindler writes that it was the first work that was written after the exertions entailed by the opera "Fidelio," and that the Master wrote it down without a break at the house of his friend, Count Brunswick. According to this the whole of the sonata would have been written during the year 1806. Ferdinand Ries, however, a pupil in whom the great Master took a friendly interest, writes as follows : " We (Beethoven and Ries) were out for a walk and lost our way so that we did not get back to Döbling, where Beethoven was staying, until eight o'clock in the evening. While we were out he had kept on humming and shouting to himself, up and down the scale, but without singing definite notes. I asked him what he was singing and he said, " A theme has occurred to me for the last movement of the sonata." When we got back and went into his room he rushed straight to the piano, without stopping to take off his hat. Then he stormed at the piano for fully an hour over the new, brilliant *Finale* of this sonata. At last he got up, was surprised to see me still there, and said, " I cannot give you any lesson to-day, I must go on with my work."

Beethoven lived at Döbling in the summers of 1803 and 1804. During one of these years the *Finale* at any rate must have been composed.

Meanwhile we have still a third account of the origin of the sonata. It is that touched upon above, about Beethoven's flight in anger from Prince Lichnowsky's house in Silesia, where an attempt was made to persuade him to play to the French officers. The Prince, who was a man of the world, wanted his protégé, the famous German musician, to sit down at the piano and entertain these distinguished gentlemen. Beethoven was unwilling from the very first; it is well known what he thought of the " Emperor " Napoleon, and now he was standing face to face with this emperor's officers, who had but lately led the army in the battle at Jena. At the dinner-table, we are told, his eyes had flashed fire when one of the officers had asked him if he played the violin, and he had not condescended to give him any other answer. When the music was about to begin he had disappeared, and when he was found and the Prince tried to prevail upon him to play, the Master was seized with downright fury. Late in the evening as it was, in rain and sleet, he left the castle, walked to the nearest town, Troppau, and there found shelter for the night in the house of the Prince's physician, Dr. Weiser. From there he sent Prince Lichnowsky a letter, containing the oft-quoted lines : " Prince, what you are, you are by accident of birth; what I am, I am by my own efforts. There have been, and always will be, thousands of princes, but there is only one Beethoven ! " *

On this occasion Beethoven took with him, amongst the possessions that he had hastily gathered together, the manuscript of the F minor sonata, which is said to bear evidence to this day of its creator's dreary and wet nocturnal walk. This happened in 1806, and Herr Bigot, Prince Rasumowsky's librarian, relates that Beethoven showed the wet-stained

* The letter is not to be found in the collection of Beethoven's letters; it is hardly likely that the Prince would have kept it ! Dr. Weiser's son is the authority for it, though he does not guarantee the exactness of the wording, but the lines quoted have the true Beethoven ring !

manuscript and drenched valise to his wife, Frau Marie Bigot, on his return to Vienna shortly after the incident. Frau Bigot was a charming woman and an excellent pianist, and Beethoven had the highest regard for her, apparently also on other grounds than those of her musical talents. She sat down at the piano, and to the Master's delight played the sonata from the damp pages, which were also covered with alterations, afterwards asking him to give her the memorable manuscript as a reward. According to Bigot's account, this was the manuscript intended for the printer; with its damp spots it is still in the possession of the family. The sonata is accordingly believed to have been finished in the autumn of 1806.

In order to reconcile these accounts with each other it has now been suggested, apparently with good reason, that Schindler, who did not become associated with Beethoven until a much later date, has confused the Lichnowskys with the Brunswicks, which is all the more probable as the sonata is dedicated to the young Count Brunswick. In any case Schindler is wrong in saying that the sonata was composed straight off " without a break." We can see from the sketch-books that Beethoven was at work on the first movement of the sonata at the same time that he was planning the opera of " Leonore " (*i.e.* " Fidelio "). There are also notes for the slow movement in this sketch-book, while a single draft for a *Finale* is quite different from the final form. These notes date from the year 1804.

There is no doubt that this mighty work, which seems to have sprung from the artist's mind whole and entire, really came into being slowly, little by little, and after engaging his imagination for at least two years, simultaneously with several other works of a totally different kind and character. This will not surprise anyone who is acquainted with Beethoven's method of creating and working. When an idea had taken shape in his mind he was able to retain it for years and to bring it out for greater elaboration when he required it. He seems, in fact, to have found it rather stimulating to be engaged simultaneously on a variety of themes, each requiring its own treatment. The mental labour of such a working out of ideas must have been considerable and it compels our admiration again and again, yet the main outlines of the work were no doubt clear to the Master from the beginning. So, too, in the case of this sonata. It may not have sprung forth " in one rush," as Schindler thought, and as we know that its forerunner, the D minor sonata, Opus 31, No. 2, did, yet its main idea and its general mood certainly arose in the year 1804, when at any rate the first two movements were finished. If we are to believe Ries's account, and we have good reasons for doing so, the themes of the last movement originated in the same year, while the final form to which they were raised probably dates from 1806—and possibly from the visit to the Lichnowsky castle.

Essentially, then, the sonata is of about the same period as the so-called " Waldstein " sonata, Opus 53. But what a contrast it forms to this predecessor! If the " Waldstein " sonata soars up into the full light of day, the " Appassionata " belongs to the dark gloom of night; if in the former we hear the voice of a joyous soul set free, the latter is the cry of a restless, harassed spirit. Both sonatas—each in its own way—are evidence of the heights to which Beethoven has risen in his art and his spiritual development. He has reached such a mastery of the technical that the material element, so to speak, no longer exists for him. He can pour out his whole soul in terms of art, the piano being his interpreter and intermediary. He had eagerly studied the executive resources of his favourite instrument, and, as we know, prevailed upon the makers of pianos to produce instruments of greater power and elasticity and of larger range than those hitherto made. If he rejoiced when he came into possession of such instruments, of fuller tone and increased compass, capable of yielding more delicate shading and a richer variety of tone colour, it was not because he wished to compose with more appreciation, brilliance or grandeur for the piano, but only because he could by these means freely and fully express the ideas that absorbed him. Here, at last, so far as it was humanly possible, he could find utterance for the music echoing in his soul. " What do you suppose I care about your wretched fiddle when the spirit speaks to me ? " he had said, with mocking humour, to Schuppanzigh, that admirable young violinist, who was the first to make his quartets ring with life. To the 'cellist Kraft, who complained that a passage in one of the quartets (from this very period) involved awkward positions, he answered brusquely, " You will have to put up with them ! " While he must, of course, have been filled with joy and satisfaction when he perceived how in that poor material implement, the piano, he could find a voice able to express the promptings of his spirit. Truly, in a sonata like this we have reached a point in Beethoven's piano works in which the technical elements—these runs and passages, these ornamentations, shakes and cadenzas—are not in any way felt to be mere external decorations, but in the highest degree an integral, inseparable part of the work of art itself. Hugo Riemann is most assuredly right when he says that " any thought of deliberate, virtuoso brilliance is a blasphemy ! "

The F minor sonata then, even in its external form, is a high-water mark amongst Beethoven's greatest achievements as a composer for the piano. Though it is one of the sonatas most frequently found on the programmes of pianists—even after the " last " sonatas were discovered, to the detriment, almost, of their predecessors—this should not confuse us. From its whole character, and because of the demands it makes in a technical sense, the sonata is justly classed amongst those which are performed not only in the home, but also in the concert-room—taking the idea of concert music in its highest sense. Unfortunately many a virtuoso mangles Beethoven's work abominably, above all by far too rapid *tempi*, intended to display the performer's brilliance, while they make havoc of the musical poem.

Let us turn, however, from these considerations of the outward aspect of the sonata to its inner essence, its spirit.

At about the same time that Beethoven conceived the idea for this Opus 57, or at any rate shortly before, he wrote at the end of a letter to the painter, Maco, " Do you paint and I will write music, so shall we live on—for ever ? Yes, perhaps for ever." It is as though he was conscious of the heights to which his genius had now soared ; as though he, as yet only half-way through his thirties, felt that he was one of the community of elect spirits of mankind, one of those who were to live for ever. This explains, perhaps, that Beethoven again for a time feels remote from, raised above communion with ordinary, earth-bound human beings, and entirely absorbed in great and wonderful inspirations. At this time he is possessed by a great need of solitude, as he was during the last years of his life. He seeks new quarters again and again, he has no permanent home ; no house shall be pointed out and mentioned as his home where it is easy to find him ; at one time the Master even had four different lodgings at his disposal at one and the same time ! Altogether he is full of a seething unrest, as though possessed by a demon, and subject to abrupt changes of mood. We see it, for instance, in the outspoken letters to his friend Breuning, in whom he confides very freely. He is capable of violent rage over trivial, everyday matters, such as questions of house-rent ; and, as he writes himself on one occasion, he is able to hide his sensitiveness on many points and to restrain himself, but if he is once roused at a time when he is in an angry mood, he explodes with more violence than anyone else. On the other hand, he is quickly brought to reason; the angry words were only the outbreak of a stormy mood, he really did not mean them, and Beethoven is seen striving to restore the good relations by means of gentle and cordial expressions of good-will.

*   *   *   *   *   *

During this period the calm of his mind is frequently disturbed by illness; he seems to have suffered from a sort of ague. He resorts to the watering-place of Baaden, but while there complains of the bad weather and of not feeling secure from the society of other people. "I must go away in order to be alone," he says, significantly indicating his state of mind. In addition to what has been told here, there were changes of mood resulting from worries and annoyances in connection with the performance of his opera "Leonora."

Some—perhaps a great deal—of the human, psychological background in the moods that find expression in the F minor sonata, can be traced back to all this. "Read Shakespeare's *Tempest!*" These words of Beethoven, whether deeply and sincerely meant or not, refer to the Opus 57 as well as to the Opus 31 that occasioned them. There is certainly a tempest like that of a Shakespearean drama in this sonata, and the storm is not external, physical, in Nature, as Czerny would explain the final movement. It is true that Beethoven loved wandering in the open country, and loved Nature most in her wildest moods, in roaring gales and driving rain, and the sonata, especially in the last movement, undoubtedly expresses something of Goethe's thought: "Dem Schnee, dem Regen, dem Sturm entgegen." Perhaps those who have said that Beethoven's imagination was stirred by sights and sounds in Nature, by the shrieking wind tearing at the trees, are right in their assertion. Judging from Ries's account, the idea for the final movement probably came to him during a walk in the country, but it is quite certain that the storm was in his own soul. It was raging in the Master's breast, moaning and wailing like the wind in Shakespeare's poetry, or in the mountains and forests of the country round Vienna.

We cannot probe to the deepest causes of this stormy mood. The outward circumstances mentioned above could only indirectly have contributed to it. It is not easy to explain why Beethoven was at this time so plunged in gloom and despair, why his mind was in such a state of turmoil. Was it the continual pain and dread caused by his failing sense of hearing? About this time Breuning writes to Wegeler on this subject: " You cannot imagine the indescribable, I might say, the *terrible* effect it has upon him that his hearing is beginning to fail." Was it a deep unsatisfied longing for requited love, memories perhaps of the rupture with the beautiful Giulietta Guicciardi, not so long before the theme of the sonata had arisen in his mind? Yet the F minor sonata, still less than the C sharp minor, does not directly speak of the moods and impulses of love. Or was it genius fretting at the chains that bound it to earth? Can it have been the solitary life which he had perforce to live, because his paths lay so far above those of ordinary men, that made him break out in a cry of despair because he was so unutterably lonely and so little understood?

We do not know. And yet we do know, because we have before us the perfect utterance of a perfect genius, and this rare and costly proof of the heights to which art can attain really tells us all that we need know.

This sonata, in which the anger and defiance of a superman find a voice, seems in a few brief moments to have sprung from the highest inspiration. Yet, as we know, it was built up, perhaps during the course of several years, by the conscious and perfectly controlled art of a master, the Master who had written, or in whose mind were growing such works as the " Kreutzer Sonata," " Fidelio," the B flat and C minor symphonies, the violin concerto, the G major piano concerto,

THERESA VON BRUNSWICK.

BEETHOVEN (c. 1817).
(*From a portrait by Klöber.*)

the rugged " Coriolan " overture, the string quartets of Opus 59, each one of which shows that it is the inspiration of a great and exalted mind.   They bear the mark of the unerring artist hand that wrote them, and some of them are partly, but only partly, kindred of the " Appassionata." We can go through this sonata phrase by phrase, bar by bar, and we shall marvel at the genius and the deliberate care with which the whole is directed to and attains the highest effect, not having one note too many or too few.   Hence its wonderful monumentality, its richness and beauty of form, that suggest to us the name of Michael Angelo, the genius to whom Beethoven is so often compared, also because of points of resemblance in character and temperament.   We can therefore apply to this sonata the words of Pascal : " Quand on voit le génie pur on est ravi—et étonné."   This is true, because there is in the rapture and astonishment an element of terror, of shock, at hearing the unmistakable, actual voice of genius speaking so openly, so terribly.   He who has not once at least felt something of this weirdness and terror is not yet fully awake to Beethoven's genius.

What has been said here about the F minor sonata might also be said about the last sonatas, in any case in a certain degree about the impassioned ones amongst them, such as the sonatas in B flat major, Opus 106, and C minor, Opus 111, and yet we seem in the " Appassionata " sonata to be more directly face to face with genius.   In the later sonatas Beethoven often speaks to us—in a style which had then become his mode of utterance—through musical phrases, or ingenious turns of expression that do not in the same degree as in the F minor sonata reveal the inner spirit to the listener.

We are told that Beethoven himself called his Opus 57 his " greatest sonata " and that it was the one he liked best to play to others.   This is very probably true.   If we are to imagine his piano-playing in its state of perfection—while he still, in

I

spite of deafness, played to others—the "Appassionata" would involuntarily occur to us in this respect.

This is the Beethoven with whom most of us are acquainted, and whom the writers of the romantic period have especially fostered : the musical genius of "Weltschmerz" that we meet in this sonata. This idea about Beethoven is no doubt one-sided and hardly so common now as it once was, nevertheless the F minor—in which there is no gleam of humour, of gaiety or of joy—is a remarkable link in the chain of sonatas, in showing so typical a side of the composer's character.

The dedication written above this sonata is a proof of how close it was to the Master's heart. Beethoven bestowed it upon Count Franz von Brunswick. The latter was one of a circle of young noblemen, enthusiastically interested in art, who had gathered about Beethoven. The composer, on his part, had the highest regard for Count Brunswick and was on terms of cordial friendship with the cultivated and musical family to which he belonged. He was a frequent guest in their home in Vienna, and during the summer stayed at their country house in Hungary. The fact that Count Franz was an able performer on the violoncello was probably a further attraction. Whether the Count's sister, Theresa, who was Beethoven's pupil in piano playing, awoke any tender feelings in him is perhaps doubtful, but it was in this home that Beethoven met Giulietta Guicciardi, a cousin of the young Brunswicks. We can understand how he would feel drawn to the family, at first because of the passion that had been awakened in him, and later because of memories held in common with them. Only once was there for a short time a break in their relations. The name of Count Franz von Brunswick on the title-page is therefore a strong indication of the value that the artist placed on the "Appassionata" sonata.

The first movement of the sonata is its most dramatic part, as the contrasts in it are the most vivid and the tension is strained to the utmost. The main theme of the movement is the great, peculiar, gliding F minor *motif*, which is strangely weird, ghostly and threatening in character. With inspired calculation this effect is doubled at the very beginning, by placing the unison *motif* two octaves apart. As a writer of keen observation remarks, the uncanny ghostliness is increased when the treble is played a little more faintly than the bass (to which the theme by its nature really belongs). It sounds as if the *motif* were followed by its own shadow. Now it is worth while pointing out that the gloomy minor voice of this theme dominated the whole movement in the first rough draft of the sonata. " Storm and darkness reign supreme, the contrast of gentleness is wanting." It was not till later that the artist found a secondary theme in A flat major, which, in spite of its gentle and soothing strains, is drawn from the leading theme in a rather unique way. It is closely related to it, both in its rhythmic and melodic features ; it is its feminine complement, one might say, formed from the masculine leading theme, as Eve was formed from the rib of Adam. Hugo Riemann calls such a resemblance between the two leading themes in a sonata " a fault in construction," but it should be easy to agree with this learned, though sometimes slightly pedantic writer, when he does not " reproach the Master " with it, especially as " the result is a unity all the greater in the whole of this tremendous movement." On the other hand, it is more difficult to understand those interpreters who profess to see something " heroic " in this second theme. It is clearly intended to produce a soothing effect after the lava-like stream at the beginning of the sonata, but there was no room for gentleness, calm or security in this piece ; the mind of its creator was too agitated, under too violent a strain. We have already heard the peculiar and mysterious " knocking " *motif* of disquiet which occurs so frequently in Beethoven's music at this time, the chief instance being that of the C minor symphony, hence called the " Symphony of Fate."

The theme is now repeated in an ingenious way; it begins ominously *pianissimo*, and already in the next bar plunges into a wild torrent of syncopated notes. We can observe how notes of anxious foreboding quiver restlessly above the pedal-point (E flat), a mode of effect usually intended—also in Beethoven's music—to show that peace and harmony have been attained, but it is not so here; the passage rather seems to indicate spasms of pain (*sforzati*) following after the first tremendous outburst and yielding, through exhaustion and resignation, to the A flat melody. It should be clear to us now that this second theme will not be able to quell the enormous powers that Beethoven has dared to call to life. Nor can it do so; the second theme is not even allowed to sing its phrase to the end, the storm again breaks into it and sweeps it aside. After some hesitating and fluttering shakes, the theme again rushes downwards, where its low rumblings express the distraction of a tormented soul.

A fight is fought out in this movement—the contrasts in it are justified; it is this fight that gives the movement life and makes it dramatic. Peace and gentleness do not conquer—but is the victory, then, to the weird terrors of night? The ending is characteristic in this respect. After the ominous, threatening knocking *motif* has grown more and more powerful it culminates at last in full chords, and the tormented soul, whose course we have followed through the whole movement, sinks down, not to rest, but to dull pain, to silent brooding; during the *pp* tremoli in the treble, keeping on like faint quiverings of the soul, the leading theme sinks back into itself more and more, vanishes into the deepest depths of the piano—at last an all but soundless *ppp* fermato chord alone remains as an eerie memory of all that has been lived through.

Then, without a pause, and as though under a compelling need—it could not be otherwise!—come the soft, deep strains of the *Andante*, sounding like an imploring prayer for peace.

With the instinct of genius Beethoven has made this part quite short. He has chosen his favourite form, variations, but he has not allowed himself to be tempted either to futile dreaming or complicated ingenuities. The whole is as simple, as concentrated, one might almost say, as anxiously humble, as required by the occasion. A virtuoso, then, cannot hope to gather any laurels in this movement, and Reinecke aptly remarks that " one must quite forget the performer, so that neither the second variation sounds like a study, nor the last one gets any trace of ' brilliance.' " The performer has to be interpreter for a soul in torment, a soul at prayer. Nothing else. But there is about the whole movement, and that is what makes it so difficult to perform, something rigid and incorporeal ; this is true both of the melody itself and of the variations upon it, and it is not without reason that the same key (D flat major) prevails through nearly the whole piece. It is evident that here we have not to do with reality. This melody and its variations do not sing of a peace attained, only of a faint trembling hope of it ; we have to do with a disembodied phantom. And listen now to the last restless displacements of the melody—after the variations are over—from one pitch to another ! Does not this make us feel the hesitation and uncertainty of the soul ? Immediately after, without having been brought to its expected and natural conclusion, the melody dies away into an impalpable *pp* arpeggio of a dissonant chord—with a long-drawn fermato that should be kept on a long time and slowly fall away into silence. Then comes the *ff* arpeggio of the same chord on higher notes that sound as if they would tear every hope of peace asunder, as with a shriek they call back the terrible reality. This dissonance, emphasised in heavily accented notes of battle—again without a pause between the movements—introduces the *Finale*.

And now—after the first flickering runs, coming down from

the highest treble, proclaiming the coming storm like warning gusts of wind in the tree-tops—an impression from Nature really seems to have inspired the Master here—the storm breaks again in the soul of the tone-poet, who did not attain to the peace he had hoped for. The *Finale* rushes on like an unrestrained torrent, flinging cascades of foam in every direction ; even for Beethoven it is unusually violent and persistent in its theme and tone. Nothing can stem the course of this raging torrent, neither the small polyphonic passages nor the syncopated and defiant staccato *motif* that flashes out for a few moments not to return again. Twice only the stream seems to sink into a trough (*pp*), but there is no sign of exhaustion, such as in the first movement. Quickly the waves rise again and break with undiminished force. This effect is characteristic of Beethoven, the tremendous excitement seems to grow and grow as in the course of writing he gets warmer and warmer and is carried away by the ardour of inspiration— in few other passages do we encounter this peculiarity of Beethoven so clearly expressed or in a form which like this so carries its hearers away. This movement overpowers us, not so much by its beauty of form as by the tremendous energy that maintains and constantly finds new expression for the " wild and impassioned character " (Riemann) of the music.

May all good spirits of art preserve this movement from becoming a virtuoso piece, a flying piano study ! It will be so preserved if the performer will quite simply follow the composer's own instructions as to *tempi*. He says Allegro *ma non troppo*. If one is guided by the latter indication the character of the movement will be preserved, and one will not be tempted to make the concluding *Presto* a breathless and indistinct *Prestissimo*—the *Presto* in which Beethoven, as never before in the whole series of sonatas, introduces a quite new *motif* at the very end, and one decisive of the conclusion of the piece. This *Presto* proclaims as though with thundering hammer strokes the firm will, the artist's energy, the defiance of destiny, that relieve the wild straining and soul-shattering despair of this music.   The character of this *Finale* is not without its share in explaining why Shakespeare's genius should be mentioned in connection with the "Appassionata" sonata.

CHAPTER XII

AFTER the great achievement of the " Appassionata " sonata, Beethoven shunned this form of art for a long while. It was as though he was afraid to take this instrument into his confidence again, so soon after the violent, the profound and agitating self-revelation which that work had been. He had composed, at about the same time as the F minor sonata, the well-known thirty-two variations in C minor—a superb unfolding of art in a form dear to him—and the beautiful G major concerto, which as a whole is bright and serene. After that the piano is silent for about two years, as a solo instrument (apart from the choral fantasia in which the piano appears in this form). When Beethoven again turns to his favourite instrument it is to find expression for quite other moods than those torn by distracting passions. Henceforth he avoids the gloom of the F minor which had meant so much to him in that work; once more only does he have recourse to this key, and then only to employ it in scherzo-form in a short middle movement (Opus 110). But during these years of the Master's life, rather uneventful outwardly, his genius creates a series of great works. His productive power had never been more sovereign.

It seems as though the joy that Beethoven found in writing for the piano had been rekindled by working at the E flat major concerto—the crown of all the concertos—for while he is engaged on it he is also at work on the sonatas Opus 78, 79 and 81, as well as on the piano fantasia Opus 77, a work not sufficiently appreciated by piano-players.

Outwardly these works came into existence at a troubled

time, a distressing and pitiable time for Austria : her armies had to retreat before the advance of the French, who in May 1809 penetrated into the suburbs of Vienna and fired upon the city. This, as we know, terrified poor Beethoven so much that he took refuge in the cellar of his brother Carl's house, and buried his head in blankets and pillows—probably, too, because the booming of the cannon was doubly painful to his diseased organs of hearing.

The three above-mentioned sonatas dating from the year 1809 are separated from the Opus 57 not only by the lapse of time, they differ from it also in character and subject. They form a sort of isolated island group in the series of the sonatas, as they are separated on the other side from those that succeeded them by a distance of six or seven years. The return to the sonata form was, therefore, somewhat transient and compact in duration—and, as said before, it occurred at an unsettled time which had its effect upon Beethoven's impressionable mind. It is no wonder, then, that this period is not the highest in his sonata composition, or that he has no deep confidences to make in these works.

The Sonata Opus 78 cannot be said to have enjoyed the particular favour or esteem, either of the executants of his piano music, or of those who have written about it. A natural cause of this will at once be found in its close proximity to such distinguished works as Opus 53 and 57. Compared to these giant trees in the Beethoven music-forest, Opus 78, even outwardly, would look like a humble, almost insignificant plant—one that in its own time was thought of but little merit—and to which even later judges of musical taste paid but slight heed ; it was, in fact, quite overlooked by such a con- noisseur of art as A. B. Marx, in his book about Beethoven's sonatas. Lenz calls it " une œuvre à laquelle la main de Beet- hoven travailla, mais non pas son génie . . . ce sont deux morceaux denués d'interêt dans une tonalité monotone et fatiguante (!)."—Czerny, on the other hand, feels that this sonata has its values, and points out " the calmness, simplicity, tenderness and devotion " in the first movement, which "should be played with the most singing expression," and the " humour and gaiety " in the last movement, adding that " the sonata differs from all earlier ones in spirit and style."

Nor have writers of a later day had *so* poor an opinion of the F sharp major sonata, and they were able to refer to the fact that it was one of the sonatas which Beethoven himself played by preference, and to his statement, which is probably authentic, that " People are always talking about the C sharp minor sonata (Opus 27), but after all, I have done better work, such as, for instance, the sonata in F sharp major." These casual words of the Master cannot, of course, be upheld before an artistic judgment—certainly the Opus 78 cannot rival the C sharp minor—and Beethoven's words, assuming that they have been correctly reported and were meant to be taken seriously, can be explained by the fact that the great Masters do not always place the highest value on their best works, but are inclined to defend the weaker ones, which have been placed by general consent in the second rank. A growling remark like the above-mentioned would fittingly come from Beethoven's lips, in irritation at the languishing enthusiasm of hysterical ladies at the wonders of the " Moonlight " sonata.*

Meanwhile the F sharp major sonata is not a work of great depth or width in subject, nor is this its aim. It must therefore not be compared to Opus 27 or 57. It is probable enough

---

* Niels W. Gade valued this little sonata highly and often played the first movement of it—playing the introductory *Adagio* with such charming effects of tone, and such great expression, that those who heard it never forgot the poetry in it. Perhaps this predilection of Gade for the sonata can be traced back to his great admiration for Felix Mendelssohn, who very probably had a great liking for this sonata, as it is a well-known fact that he placed a high value on Opus 90, and greatly preferred it to the later sonatas. The beauty of tone in Gade's playing may have been an echo of the rendering of Mendelssohn, the greater artist in piano-playing.

that it gives some impression of Beethoven's improvisations at the piano, as it has particularly been asserted that the contemporary Fantasia Opus 77 does. He sits down to the piano, the fine, wildly beautiful head with its wealth of bushy hair bent over the keyboard—in the attitude described by contemporaries of the Master, when playing during his later years and when his hearing was failing more and more. While his mind is filled with introspective dreaming, his hands charm forth from the instrument that wondrously beautiful and simple musical idea, so delicate in its fragrance and so visionary in its tone, which forms the introduction of the sonata, and which indicates the F sharp major mood, though the idea itself is not pursued further or developed more fully in the subsequent *Allegro*.* The " calm and tender " movement joined to this introduction is a fine and delicate play of tone, rather than a strictly worked out or richly varied musical form : it expresses a gentle and balanced state of mind, and is ingenious and sparing in its use of the tone effects to be found in the piano. In so far it might well be placed beside an improvisation and called a forerunner of the last sonatas, especially of the new style of the E major and A flat major. In the *Finale* the tone is gayer and freer; the play of tone, which is perhaps the best term for the subject of this sonata, develops in a whimsical, as Czerny says, a " humoristic " way, though there is no question here of the bold and grand humour that we encounter in greater works

---

* Hugo Riemann, in his often admirably penetrating analyses of the sonatas, is inclined to call this *Adagio* a separate movement, and maintains that its theme is found in a corresponding passage in the bass at the end of the *Allegro*, but it is difficult to agree with his opinion that this is " more than a matter of chance." A composer, and at any rate a Beethoven, would hardly be so calculating. Riemann also points out that the closing figure in the introduction is a well-known " Mannheim

manner."  Would this really be " more than a matter of

chance " ?

or in sonata movements in which Beethoven's mind really flashes humour. The leading idea in the movement seems like a playfully dropped question and answer; it does not contain any amorous feeling or other passionate emotion.

The sonata has only these two movements. That is quite reasonable, or one might say logical, for the whole sonata is limited in mood, neither demanding great room nor long time for development. The first movement : the *Adagio Cantabile* introduction and the succeeding *Allegro*, which is expressly defined *ma non troppo*, is of such a character that a slow piece is not needed. The last movement can at the same time take the part of a *Scherzo* and a *Finale ;* being thus related to the *Finales* of Opus 14, No. 2, 26 and 54, but it is more graceful, more delicate, more gently playful than any of these. Each movement ends with a *Coda* which is well worth noticing. Beethoven's master hand has rarely drawn with so few lines such a shy, lingering grace as that of the close of the first movement, or such a dainty gaiety as the *Coda* of the *Finale*.

While Beethoven in his F minor sonata, as though in an inspired frenzy, modelled an imposing colossal statue like one of Michael Angelo's, he has in this F sharp major sonata produced a delicately chased little Tanagra figure—small enough to be held in the hand, and, if one may say so, of just the kind to be fondled carefully by the tender and understanding hand of a musician. The concert-room is not the place for this sonata, and fortunately it is hardly ever heard there. The tempestuous runs, the mighty chords, the flashing accents are gone; it is all like a filigree of sound, breathed softly from the keyboard—even a Hans von Bülow calls some parts of it " precarious." How delicate and ethereal is this play of tone can be seen from the fact that not only are Beethoven's famous and thundering basses entirely and necessarily absent, but the whole subject is placed in a higher register than that generally used in the earlier sonatas, the treble clef replacing the bass clef in these two short movements not less than sixteen times in the first *Allegro*, twenty times in the *Finale*, while the left hand plays, roughly speaking, about a fourth part of the first movement in the treble. This gives the sonata some of its peculiar character; and the entire piano treatment— where a single section with the dynamic contrasts might suggest an organ with its stronger and weaker manuals—the alert attention to shadings in attack, the efforts to maintain a particular mood in each movement, causing the counter theme to retreat into the background—may, as Czerny says, be called a "new style" in Beethoven's piano music. Can it have been due to this circumstance that Beethoven accorded it a particularly high place among its sister sonatas? It can hardly be said, though, that the F sharp major sonata denotes a conscious change of artistic aim. Just as there is in its subject no trace of struggle, doubt or unrest, it does not seem to have come into the world after severe travail. It is one of the somewhat few sonatas for which no sketches have been found—and this again would seem to indicate its improvised origin. The sonata as it is, is one of those which shows us another Beethoven than that genius of "Welt-schmerz" which a man like Romain Rolland, among the newer writers, has described in a rather one-sided way in a popular and widely read book about the Master.

The sonata is dedicated to Theresa von Brunswick. From what has been discussed above one would like to think that it has grown from an improvisation played on a serene and beautiful day at the country seat of the Brunswicks, Beethoven's friends in Hungary. The sonata is generally believed to have been composed there, and Thayer is of opinion, as has been remarked, that it was this sonata, and not the "Appassionata," that was written (according to Schindler) "at one stroke," in Count Brunswick's house. With a little imagination this summer music of F sharp major suggests the soft breezes stirring the white lace curtains and streaming into the bright and lofty drawing-room with the garden view, in which are heard the singing strains of the piano.

The dedication has given rise to speculation and writing. Students who, like Thayer, have wanted to make Theresa von Brunswick both Beethoven's fiancée and the " immortally beloved" to whom the letter mentioned in dealing with Opus 27, No. 2, was directed, have, of course, noted the Master's appreciative words about the F sharp major with satisfaction, while Giulietta's champions have pointed out how little value contemporary and later connoisseurs placed upon this so-called " Theresa sonata." If Beethoven's feelings for the two women are to be gauged by the sonata which he dedicated to each of them, there can be no doubt as to which of the ladies carries off the prize ! Meanwhile there is no particularly solid ground for thinking that there were tender relations, or that even a definite understanding existed between Beethoven and Theresa. Evidence of this has been pointed out in a phrase occurring in a letter from Beethoven to the young lady's brother : " Kiss your sister Theresa for me and tell her I am afraid I shall become ' great ' without her having contributed to it with a monument." These words were written in 1807, when Countess Theresa, or rather Theresia, was already twenty-nine years old, and they were doubtless only an Austrian form of courtesy and friendship ; in everyday talk the phrase " Küss die Hand " was not taken so literally ! The concluding words are a humorous allusion to the craze of the wealthy and aristocratic of those days—and so probably also the Brunswicks—for erecting statues, or perhaps mostly memorial tablets, in their houses or gardens, in honour of those whom they idolised most in the world of art. It is scarcely probable that the words had anything to do with a tender passion.

From portraits of her, Theresa Brunswick is known to us as a handsome woman with noble classical features, but a somewhat cold expression, and wearing the Roman costume so much in favour at the time and also characteristic of her own taste. We know that she was a competent pianist and that she had the highest regard for Beethoven both as an artist and a man. She presented him with her portrait with the words : " To the rare genius, the great artist, the good man, from T. B." But no one is justified in drawing further conclusions from these few facts and attributing serious feelings for the Countess to Beethoven.

Moreover Theresa von Brunswick had at the age of sixteen made a vow never to marry—romantic as she seems to have been—and she kept her vow. She lived so late as 1861 in a secular convent or community of ladies of rank in Brünn. After her death the contention about her relations with Beethoven led to the production of her diary, in which she has given a very vivid picture of the Master and their first associations with each other :

" Beethoven could never be induced to comply with a mere request from us " (it concerned his giving lessons to Theresa and her sister Josephine), " but if we would undertake to climb to the third storey by the narrow winding stairs at St. Peter's Square * and pay him a visit, the result was guaranteed. Then it was like this. We went like school-girls, with Beethoven's sonatas for piano and violin and violoncello under our arms, into his roon. The dear, immortal Louis van Beethoven was very kind and as courteous as *he* could be."

" After the exchange of a few compliments he made me sit down at his piano (which was out of tune) and I began at once, singing the violin or the 'cello part to the music—

* The old-fashioned stone winding stairs in Viennese houses, of which there was still one left at the end of the last century, leading up to the flat in which Johannes Brahms lived.

and playing quite nicely.   He was so delighted that he promised to come every day to the ' goldenen Greif.' "   (Probably the town residence of the Brunswicks.)   This was in March 1799 (Theresa was then twenty-one).   " He came frequently, but instead of staying an hour until twelve o'clock, he often stayed until four or five and did not grow tired of keeping my fingers turned inwards or of bending them.   That splendid man must have been very pleased with me, for he did not miss coming once during sixteen days—and by that time we had formed a sincere and cordial friendship which lasted to the end of his life."

Would it not seem that these few lines give the true, unadorned relation between the great composer and the young Countess ? The amorous feelings attributed to this friendship are not easy to find in Theresa von Brunswick's simple and natural account.

THE ARCHDUKE RUDOLPH.

CHAPTER XIII

THE little sonata (or sonatina) in G major, Opus 79, does not, certainly, take a high place among the sonatas surrounding it, but there is no reason to ignore it in an account of the sonatas, as some writers have done. So much the less because it is undoubtedly not, as some have said, an early work which has been revived, but one that has been created during this period. Outlines for the first movement can be found in a sketch-book of 1809 together with the plans for considerable works like the string quartet Opus 74, the E flat major piano concerto, the music for "Egmont," etc. Besides, the fact that Beethoven had first sketched out the beginning of the sonata in another key before he decided on G major, would seem to be an indication that it was not an old idea which was now taken up afresh. On the other hand, the title of the sonata, which already appears in the sketch-book, *Sonate facile*, shows that the small opus was intended from the first to be a piece of music easy to play and easy to dispose of, or to be used for teaching purposes. Though it is not unreasonable to compare it with the small sonatas of Opus 49, this cannot be done without some reservations. The Opus 79 belongs to a later period, and although modest in appearance and extent, with its normal three movements it is a broad and elaborate work, even though one would not care to be so subtle as Hans von Bülow, who in the style of a phrase or two would see an annunciation of the sonatas of the "last period" to come so soon after.

The first movement re-echoes the folk-music of Vienna

more directly than any other sonata. The "Ländler" and waltz are gaily and lightly mirrored in this music and the composer himself has alluded to them by heading it "Alla tedesca." This leads Hans von Bülow to maintain that Beethoven's "Ländler" music is more inspired, that is, more "manly" than that of Franz Schubert. Is there really any ground for this assertion, or any reason at all to pit the two masters against each other in this small field of art? If one did, one might rather point out that the "Ländler" of Schubert express unadulterated Viennese gaiety in a graceful and charming *laisser aller* manner, while Beethoven has translated the classic Viennese dance into a more academic language. A premonition of Mendelssohn's *Lieder ohne Worte* has been found in the *Andante*, and Beethoven's later piano works have undoubtedly been decisive in the music of the romantic composers for the piano, nor can a melodic resemblance between the beginning of the *Andante* and one of the *Lieder* in the same tonality (G minor) be denied. Yet an attentive ear will almost certainly perceive the difference between this artless *Andante* and the conscious emotionalism and drawing-room tone of the Mendelssohn *Lieder*.

The little sonata, which concludes with a merry and graceful *Vivace*, was most likely not of much importance in Beethoven's life and work. It is significant, in this connection, that it was issued without any dedication.

The significance that may be found in such a dedication, and its importance in understanding the work that carries it, is shown in the next sonata, Opus 81 in E flat major. This sonata is dedicated to the Archduke Rudolph, and this circumstance is the key to understanding it.

The Archduke Rudolph was one of the very few who could venture to call himself Beethoven's pupil; according to Ferdinand Ries the only one besides Ries himself. The sonata

movements are headed : " Das Lebewohl," " Die Abwesen-
heit," " Das Wiedersehen " ; * and it has generally been called
the " Lebewohl Sonata " after the subject of the first movement, sometimes also " Les Adieux," but with a delicate ear for
language, Beethoven protested against this French heading
(an amendment by an enterprising publisher), because, as he
said, " Lebewohl " and " Les Adieux " are not quite the
same ; the first expresses an intimate leave-taking between
two friends, the other sounds more official. Perhaps the
circumstance that Beethoven so frequently heard this farewell greeting in Vienna from the lips of the unpopular French
officers had a share in his dislike of the expression.

Now, if one did not know better, it would be very tempt-
ing to look for amorous moods in this musical work : the
separation of two lovers, their longing for each other and
the joy of reunion. Strange to say, even a man like A. B.
Marx, who as a Beethoven biographer was acquainted with
the dedication and its origin, describes and interprets the
subject of the sonata as though it were a question of a love
affair : " Momente aus dem Leben eines liebenden Paares." †
In the first and last movements he hears the duets of the
male and female voices—it bothers him a little, but only a
little, that sometimes the two must be supposed to be singing
in four voices !—and perceiving that there is no real pain or
passion at the moment of parting, he praises the Master's
" true restraint " ! ‡   Others have regarded the sonata in the
same light, and in the *Finale* even a Hans von Bülow soars to
the heights of hearing an annunciation of the passionate

* The Farewell, The Absence, The Return.
† " Incidents in the life of a pair of lovers."
‡ Behnke, the editor of the new edition of Marx's Beethoven biography, defends
him on the assumption that Beethoven wrote or sketched out the sonata (*i.e.* in
reality only the first movement) *before* the Archduke left Vienna in May 1809. If
there seems to be a point here that has not been or cannot be explained, it is definitely
put in the background by the fact that Beethoven *himself* gave the sonata the above-
mentioned sub-titles and dedicated it to the Archduke.

meeting of " Tristan and Isolde " in the second act of Richard
Wagner's music drama, although a sound and natural perception, and an artistic understanding of Beethoven's music
can find in it none of the sensual and passionate, the over-
excited eroticism which Wagner has reproduced in *Tristan*.
Here it is that the dedication is on the side of the wholesome
view of the sonata.   There is not the slightest suggestion of
erotic feelings in it, not even of any passionate emotion at
parting or reunion.   It is quite simply a farewell greeting
from Beethoven to his distinguished pupil, and we know
from the manuscript that " Das Lebewohl " was composed
(or completed) on May 4, 1809, " at the departure of His
Imperial Highness, the honourable Archduke Rudolph " ; while
the last piece, written January 30, 1810, is concerned with his
" Ankunft " (arrival).

In a letter to the publishers, Breitkopf and Härtel, Beethoven calls this sonata " greatly characteristic." This is a
further indication of the angle from which it ought to be
regarded.   It is a work having for its object the reproduction
of character (psychology) like that which Haydn also attempted
in some of his sonatas.   But a musician of such delicate perception as Beethoven would hardly use the expression " characteristic " about a piece of music on a subject of amorous
emotion.

Using the term in a distinguished sense the sonata may then
be called a work " written for a special occasion," and the character of the music shows it.   This is not a tone poem produced
by a mind under great pressure ; it does not contain an artist's
confession of faith ; it is not the broad and mellow painting
of an ecstatic ; rather is it a delicate and daintily chased
farewell and welcome, of the kind that might in those days
be found in the autograph book of a friend or benefactor.
They could be written without much emotion, and at the
mere cost of a little thought and wit ; such as the first move-

BETTINA BRENTANO.

BEETHOVEN (*c.* 1814).
(*From an engraving by Hoefel after the
drawing by Louis Letronne.*)

ment, which is a graceful and ingenious play on the word
" Lebewohl " expressed by means of the so-called horn-fifths.
It is quite in Beethoven's manner that he bids his depart-
ing friend farewell, not only in the first bars and in the
subsequent ones, in which the three notes are the leading
ones and are distinctly prominent, but that he varies them
here and there, letting them occur, now in a slightly sad
accent, now a little playfully, until the delightful close, in
which the sigh of the last farewell seems to fade away linger-
ingly through the air—until the two f chords put an end to
emotion. And in the last movement : the soaring joy of
reunion, a couple of bars that seem to picture a gay waving
of a handkerchief in welcome—bars that might perhaps for a
moment turn one's thoughts to Isolde's greeting before the
extinction of the torchlights—and then a gay, almost frisky
joy in having the absent one back again ; in a second theme
that is like a boyish hopping about and clapping of hands.
Deeper feelings are not uttered in these two movements.
When we are acquainted with the event that occasioned this
Opus, we can understand that Beethoven could not have been
inspired by them.

The casual origin of the sonata also explains that Beethoven
did not display all his genius in its execution. This work, in
its own way, has some of the same offhand, improvised stamp
as its predecessor, Opus 78, and so far the two works illumine
each other. Note, for instance, notwithstanding the greater
compass of the Opus 81, the comparatively short modulation
part compared to that of the " Appassionata " sonata.

There is a notable kinship between Opus 78 and 81, in which
Beethoven is seen to be less occupied with great and impressive
subjects, than in ranging with masterly ease over a light and
transparent play of tone. For it really means that this little
island group (as it was called in a previous chapter) in the
series of the sonatas forms a transition to a period in Beet-

hoven's work in which the creative impulse is waning. The next subsequent years produce altogether only a small number of new works. Not until three or four years later does the desire to create again gather force, partly urged on by exterior (political) events, and in 1814 Beethoven, as we know, experiences a " glorious " year. Yet it is a question of only a brief flickering-up—several rather dull years follow, and apart from the single E minor sonata Opus 90, seven whole years from the appearance of Opus 81 were to pass before Beethoven again added to—and closed—the glorious series of his piano sonatas.

The change in Beethoven's productive power alluded to here and beginning about the year 1809 cannot, as Thayer has pointed out, be attributed to his increasing years. It was too sudden and unmistakable for that, and besides, Beethoven was still in the full vigour of manhood. For the sake of continuity and because of the light which it throws forward on the succeeding sonata works, a few points which may have been decisive shall be noted here. Beethoven's letters of this period contain exclamations of despair, the evidence of a mind distracted almost to the point of disease. Here are one or two examples: in 1810 to his friend, Dr. Wegeler: ". . . (of late years) I have been dragged by force into the life of the world; I have not yet seen any result from it, rather the contrary—yet who can remain unaffected by the storms from without ? And yet I should be happy, perhaps the happiest of mankind, if this demon had not made its dwelling in my ears. If I had not read somewhere that no one must of his own free will quit this life, so long as he can still perform a good deed, I should long since have ceased to exist—and by my own hand. Ah, life is so beautiful, but for me it is for ever poisoned ! " Or in 1808 to Baron von Gleichenstein, Beethoven's young friend during these years: " I must again look for communion, then, within my own breast, there is nothing for me from without; no, friendship and kindred feelings have caused me nothing but wounds. Be it so, then, there is no exterior happiness for you, poor Beethoven, you must create it all within yourself—you will find friends only in the ideal world."

Here, then, we see the causes of his depressed state of mind : despair at the demon which rages more and more in the Master's ears; disappointment when he again made approaches to the world about him—social life—giving up the solitude to which he fled for a time in order to work in peace; a disappointment caused not only by his influential friends, but still more by frustrated plans of marriage. For at this time Beethoven was entertaining such plans—he might then have become " one of the happiest of mankind,"—and his friend wounds him because he will not help and support him in the projected plan. It occupied Beethoven's mind so much, that in the letter to Wegeler he urgently requested the latter to procure his birth certificate in Bonn; " the sooner you can send it to me, the greater will be my obligation." Whom did Beethoven now wish to marry? It is not known for certain. It was at one time believed to be the handsome but superficial and quite young Theresa Malfatti, daughter of Beethoven's physician and sister-in-law to the young Baron von Gleichenstein. It is now generally thought that his dreams of matrimony were concerned with the celebrated Bettina Brentano, that remarkable, gifted and fantastic-romantic writer, whose artist enthusiasm for Beethoven was extraordinary to the verge of ecstasy, as she herself has shown in her book, *Goethe's Correspondence with a Child,* which must not be read as a historical document, however, in so far as it is concerned with Beethoven's person and the conditions of his life. Judging from the information acquired by later research, one is led to be somewhat sceptical with regard to Bettina's version of her relations with Beethoven, and this consequently also places his matrimonial plans in a doubtful light. But there can be no doubt that the shipwreck of these plans—whatever the reason, or with whomsoever they were concerned—was a great blow to Beethoven and added to his despondency and weariness, and there is no indication that he found any relief this time in his art.

Beethoven's mind was also oppressed and embittered by the political state of affairs at home and abroad—" who would not feel the effect of the storms from without ? "—at the degradation of his adopted country. The improvement afterwards was therefore almost one of over-excitement, and the conditions prevailing in the country, which tormented his spirit of freedom, were a further source of annoyance and anxiety at the general economical distress. On this latter point his care gradually reached an acute stage, verging on the morbid.

The Archduke Rudolph, to whom the sonata is dedicated, was born in 1788, and was therefore much younger than Beethoven. He was brother to the reigning Emperor and, like so many members of this royal family—we need mention only the two illustrious ladies, Maria Theresa and Marie Antoinette—was gifted with a remarkable musical talent ; in common with contemporary members of the aristocracy in Vienna he was fond of showing his interest in music by giving musicians his patronage. He had received his training as a pianist and amateur composer from Tayber, the old Court musician, but the grounding he had obtained in these lessons was termed " poor " by Beethoven—though this remark may have been due to bad humour at the time. In any case Beethoven's teaching, which is said to have begun about 1804, must have worked wonders, for later on we find in the Master's letters expressions of unbounded enthusiasm at the musical productions of his pupil—so strong, indeed, that one slightly doubts his sincerity.

Beethoven made an exception in overcoming his dislike of teaching, being pleased to have the enthusiastic young Prince as an adherent, and hardly unaffected by his exalted social position. Although it could not over-awe the republican spirit of the artist, he would not fail to see its practical value. The relations between the Prince and himself continued until his death—and nothing is known of any real breach between them during all these years. It is now generally believed that the extracts which Beethoven (about 1809) was engaged in making from works on the theory of music, and which Seyfried has edited as a sort of forgery as *Beethoven's Studies*, were meant to be used in teaching the Archduke, and to form the foundation of the lessons. It can hardly be supposed that Beethoven, who had no experience as a teacher, could with his temperament be an ideal or even systematic guide, but there can, of course, be no doubt about the enormous influence of such an artist personality, or the significance of consultations with him on music.

To Beethoven this relationship of master and pupil gradually became a burden and a nuisance, which he did not conceal and would have liked to throw off. Yet it would not have been either easy or wise to break with the Archduke. For two reasons. Partly because Rudolph was not only his pupil, but at the same time his unfailing friend (whose soft, ingratiating voice, by the way, Beethoven was able to hear longest), and with a certain pride Beethoven points this out when writing (to his lawyer) that " the Archduke treated him more as a friend than as a servant," a phrase that in a brief formula defines the difference between the eighteenth century, with the social position of such famous Masters as Haydn and Mozart, and the new century that had just dawned. Partly because, in spite of everything, there was in Beethoven's blood an inherited reverence for a royal personage. What did it not mean, to be an anointed king or emperor in those days, and here was a near relative of one ! And what humble and humiliating years, in an intense feeling of dependence on the Regent, had Beethoven not lived through in Bonn! He would hardly attain to complete freedom from this feeling towards the Prince—this at any rate must explain the more than respectful tone in the letters to the Archduke.

Beethoven's relations with the Archduke, then, had a certain doubleness. Opposed to those almost servile letters and notes there are oral and written utterances to others which show ill-will, annoyance and bitterness in regard to his tutorship and his dependence on the Archduke. According to Bettina Brentano, though she is not a very reliable witness, Beethoven, for instance, was indignant at having to wait in an ante-room at the Archduke's, and is said to have given vent to his opinion in unmistakable terms, that this was not the way to treat a Beethoven. To a Swiss visitor Beethoven declared that " teaching was tiresome work; he had only one pupil and would like to get rid of him if he could." That was the Archduke. Once, when he was asked whether Rudolph played well, he answered with a short laugh, " Yes, when he is in good form," adding that he has sometimes had to strike him across his fingers during the lessons. In speaking of their relationship Beethoven even went so far as writing to Ries (who has left out the words in his *Biographical Notes*) : " My unfortunate connection with this Archduke is almost bringing me to beggary." The outburst dates from the later years and was caused by rage at having to waste time and thought on a tutorship, which—in spite of Beethoven's revolt and anger—was of course arranged to suit the wishes and convenience of the pupil. Having to stand at attention like this and to be the butt of highly trained courtiers with their finicking rules of etiquette into the bargain (for there are records of this also), must have ruffled Beethoven's feelings intensely.

On the other hand, Beethoven could mention the Arch-

duke's name " with a childlike reverence such as for no other."
And undoubtedly he would be deeply touched when the
Archduke, in common with the still younger Count Kinsky
and Prince Lobkowitz, who was slightly older, drew up that
reversion in which, in order to secure Beethoven to their own
country of Austria (a remunerative offer of an appointment
as conductor of the Court orchestra had been made to him
from Cassel by King Jérôme), they guaranteed him an annual
allowance of 4000 gulden, of which 1500 were guaranteed
by the Archduke (there does not seem to have been any
question of solidarity amongst the guarantors), " so that the
necessities of life need not embarrass him or hamper his
great genius." * Beethoven received the document at the
very time we have reached in the account of the sonatas. On
March 1, 1809, he formally endorses it : " Received from the
hands of H.R.H. the Archduke Rudolph." But this cup of
joy was also to be mingled with gall. In 1811 the unfortunate
letters patent were already issued, by which it was hoped
that the finances of the much-exhausted empire might be
re-established. It reduced paper currency to one-fifth of its
value and Beethoven's prospects of a security from care in the
future were considerably lessened, although the Archduke
Rudolph, at Beethoven's request, generously consented to
keep his contribution up to the whole of its original value.
But it *was* a bitter pill for Beethoven to swallow, in regard
to this, that " the Court entourage, in spite of all apparent
friendship, express their opinion that my claims are unjust !!!!!
Ah, Heaven, help me to bear it ; I am no Hercules who can
help Atlas to sustain the world or even do it instead of him. . . .
I cannot go on living *here* much longer in this shameful way !
Art, persecuted art, can find a refuge everywhere ! " Was

* It has been thought, perhaps with some reason, that the handsome object of the
donation was that Beethoven might be spared the disappointment it would have
been for him, deaf as he was, to be made a " Kapellmeister " (conductor of a Court
orchestra).

he thinking then of the E flat concerto, which immediately before these lines were written had been a failure at the performance in Vienna, but in Leipzig had roused the audience to an enthusiasm which could hardly remain content to show its appreciation and pleasure in the ordinary way ?—Later on Prince Kinsky's unreliability, and soon after, his sudden death, followed by Prince Lobkowitz being declared incapable of managing his affairs, led the matter of the allowance into lengthy and distressing lawsuits.

In 1820 the Archduke was made Prince Archbishop of Olmütz. It is probable that this promotion had led Beethoven to entertain further expectations. In these, too, he was disappointed, the Archduke took no steps in his favour, but, as said before, their friendly relations continued, and all the dedications, through which Beethoven has bestowed immortality on the Archduke's name, would seem to show that the friendship meant something to him. Besides the " Lebewohl " sonata there are the G major and E flat major piano concertos, the piano trio Opus 97, the violin sonata Opus 96, the *Missa solemnis*, the great " Hammerklavier " sonata Opus 106 and the sonata Opus 111, and finally the " great fugue," Opus 133. To no other name has Beethoven so often given the honour of a place on the title-page of his works—and, as it is seen, on some of his greatest.

It cannot be asserted that the Archduke, in his relations with Beethoven—which have been dealt with at greater length here, as they are also concerned with the Sonata Opus 106— showed his appreciation of the glorious gifts which made his name immortal, by making a return. His great admiration of the Master, notwithstanding his charming manner and disposition, did not prevent him, as one writer has said, from sometimes showing himself as the ruler to his famous teacher, and in a deeper sense he neither understood nor valued at his true worth the man or the genius Beethoven. So little, indeed,

Heiligenstadt, near Vienna.

did the Archduke think of this, that during Beethoven's last years in Vienna he would still make claims upon the ageing and ailing Master daily for two or three hours, so that Beethoven was afterwards too worn out to do any other work. The discontented remarks that he often let fall about his royal pupil and friend can easily be understood.   To compare this relationship with that of Goethe and Charles Augustus, or even with that of J. S. Bach and Prince Leopold, cannot be done, let loyal German biographers say what they will.

CHAPTER XIV

THERE is only one stage more before we reach that of the "last sonatas." For nearly five years Beethoven had forsaken the piano, then he wrote this one sonata in E minor. It is numbered Opus 90 and was composed in 1814, the date, August 16, most probably being that of its completion. Like the sonatas mentioned in the foregoing chapters, it stands alone, separated from them by a lapse of five years, and from the next in the series, Opus 101, by more than one year.

Does this circumstance contribute to our appreciation of this two-movement sonata? Perhaps it does. For in what other ways was Beethoven's mind occupied at this time? The sketch-books contain an outline of the sonata (especially the first part) facing a reconstruction of " Fidelio." It was at this time that the Master's friends thought that the unsuccessful opera should be given its rightful place, now that he was once more a celebrity in Vienna, and seen again in Viennese society. In his joy at the fall of " the tyrant " and the re-establishment of the country of his choice, he submitted to being fêted, not only by the Viennese, but also by a great number of royal personages assembled in Vienna for the great Peace Congress. The Beethoven with whom we are now to become acquainted is rather different from the one we have hitherto known; this is the Beethoven who composed that noisy piece : " Wellington's Victory," or " The Battle of Vittoria," dedicated to the Prince Regent of England, afterwards George IV. For political reasons this piece naturally became more popular than any of his other works and was published in many different arrangements. This is the Beethoven who wrote that very insignificant choral work, " Der glorreiche Augenblick," as a tribute to no less than three sovereigns, the Austrian, Russian and German. This is the composer of the chorus, " Germania, Germania," to be sung in a " patriotic " musical play at the Kärntnerthor-Theatre. Further, it was he who presented the Empress Elisabeth Alexievna of Russia with a polonaise for piano, composed during the same year, 1814. This Beethoven rather enjoys the adulation of emperors and kings, and he tries, though without much success, to make the most of this favourable state of affairs from a financial point of view, but it is only fair to state that in this he was acting under exterior influence. In all the simplicity of his artist soul Beethoven sunned himself in this radiant light, not reflecting that it was transient and largely a matter of chance. Once the Congress was over his brilliant fame would vanish and the memory of him fade from the minds of the celebrated and for the most part rather worldly guests of this Congress, through which they danced and feasted their way without any thought of the value of Beethoven as a man or an artist. Disappointment was in store for him. Even his gay Viennese soon deserted him and followed quite a different, anything but " Germanic " taste.

Now the piano sonata Opus 90 is the only work produced by Beethoven at this time, so to speak, without any exterior impulse. It is the only one to which " the world " had not enticed or urged him, the only one in which he has retired into himself, to quiet communion with his true, inner spirit. No publisher, no impresario, no theatre manager or arranger of festivals was waiting to receive the Master's finished work and use it to his own advantage, nor was it intended for any royal patron.

We may regard this sonata, then, the only independent lyrical work of this period, in which the Master was caught in a worldly vortex that absorbed his energy, as in a way a confession. Its opening bars seem to be a direct indication that the Master is seeking to tear himself away with a wrench from all the enticing glitter of the world that held him enthralled for a while, and that he has "come to himself." The first *Allegro* tells of this struggle to return to his better self, of changing moods of a courageous spirit, of self-confidence, resignation and timidity. The movement is characterised as much by its inner feeling as by its musical beauty of form; we hear again Beethoven's own language, to which he has returned after having spoken in strange tongues. The sketchbooks, too, seem to show that from the outset Beethoven was conscious that the sonata was to be made up of these contrasts. We find, immediately after the outline for the beginning of the sonata, without any intervening passage, the following bars :

the word "Ende" being written above them. This would seem to be a rarity in Beethoven's numerous sketches, and shows that at the very moment when the idea took shape in his mind, those beautiful bars with their luminous soaring notes,

followed immediately by sad resignation, were to be the close
of the sonata.   He has even laid a particular stress on these bars
by carefully providing this first outline of them with expression
marks—a somewhat rare occurrence in the sketch-books;
indeed he has written a *poco ritenuto*, which was omitted in the
printed sonata, probably because he felt it was so obvious that
directions for it were unnecessary.

Yet, though the movement closes on a note of resignation in
these final bars, it contains no feeling of emptiness or aridity,
in spite of the " drop " to the lower octave; still less is there
any of that " Nirvana mood " that some would find in the later
works of Beethoven.   This ending forms the natural passage
to a final movement—a *Rondo* with the significant additional
directions in *German :* " nicht zu geschwind und sehr singbar
vorgetragen "—in which a gentle peacefulness, a quiet feeling
of interior happiness finds expression.   This movement
distinctly expresses a mood of restfulness, or symbolises it by
the continual return of the lovely, singing melody, always in
the same form, in key, in rhythm and in harmonies.   This
monotony, which has often been unjustly criticised as wearisome
or " long," forms a picture of entire harmony and repose; its
effect is almost that of a soothing cradle-song.   Many later
composers of the romantic school have modelled their instrumental or vocal lyrics upon it.   How many are there not, to
whom Schubert and his " Bächlein " will be recalled on hearing
this melody.   And yet—there is a difference, not very palpable,
it is true, but perceptible to a delicate ear.   Perhaps it is best
explained as consisting in this : that in the case of Beethoven
we have to do with absolute music, music that is self-sufficient,
while the romantic composer's music is descriptive, it is not
quite self-sufficient, it is music, so to speak, with a co-ordinate
intention.

Now, when you play or hum this beautiful, simple melody,
which seems to have arisen as spontaneously as a folk-song, you

L

will perhaps be surprised to learn that it first arose in Beethoven's mind in a less perfect form, viz. :

a series of notes which he, with his genius, knew how to re-shape and convert into that immortal melody by a slight change in the up-beat and the addition of one note.

Hans von Bülow has made the apt remark that the sonata, which consists only of these two movements, should be played respectively as though " spoken " and " sung." It is a musical mode of expression related to that with which we have met in the *Allegretto* in Opus 14 (and which, as it happens, is also in E minor).

Altogether the sonata belongs in a marked degree to the " intimate " ones, to those that have no message for the concert-room, where it is, in fact, seldom heard.

If, in view of the foregoing remarks, this sonata is to be regarded as the Master's abrupt farewell to the deceits and vain pomps of this world, and as his quiet surrender to a purer and nobler world of the spirit, then it naturally leads on to the " last sonatas." Like a beautiful gate through which is seen a bright firmament, it is an entrance to all that is remote from a world which these last works would forsake and abandon.

There was, in earlier days, a more earthly and commonplace interpretation of this E minor sonata, but it was not a very plausible one. It is connected with the dedication with which Beethoven sent it forth into the world. The sonata is dedicated to Count Moritz Lichnowsky, a brother to the Count Carl mentioned earlier. He was a talented musician, and a pupil of Mozart himself, a fact which no doubt increased Beethoven's interest in him. There is every proof, not least in the letters that have been preserved, that the relations between the composer and the Count were friendly and confidential, even though the suspicion and strong independence of the former may at times have caused difficulties.

The sonata was now interpreted on the strength of this dedication, and on the following grounds. The Count, who had been divorced from his first wife, and had but lately married a young and beautiful Viennese dancer, is said to have asked Beethoven what the sonata meant, and to have received the answer, given with " a boisterous laugh," that the first movement represented " a struggle between the head and heart," the second " a conversation with the beloved," this being a supposed allusion to the Count's matrimonial affairs. This at once led to an interpretation that was very much in favour for some time, of Beethoven's music, as expressing a struggle between two principles, and it was now applied to this sonata.

Nevertheless, the dedication seems to have meant more to Beethoven than a mere matter of courtesy. At any rate he writes in September 1814, to Count Moritz : ". . . in order that you may not think that I have taken this step with ulterior thoughts of advantage or the like, I wish to tell you that a sonata of mine will soon be published and be dedicated to you. I had intended to surprise you with it, the dedication having long since been meant for you, but your letter of yesterday " (which, as Beethoven says at the beginning of his letter, " heaps kindnesses upon him ") " causes me to reveal it to you now . . . but I should feel very grieved if you thought of anything like a gift, as that would be to misjudge my good intention, and I cannot but decline anything of that kind." It is clear, then, that Beethoven had the dedication of this sonata greatly at heart ; he had long been looking forward to it, and he was very anxious that the Count should not think he was following the usual custom and bestowing his gift in order to receive something in return. In making this dedication Beethoven wished to honour his friend, not his art patron, but there is no reason to conclude from this that he would be so coarse and tactless as to depict the Count's private affairs in the sonata. The sardonic laughter of the Master when he gave his supposed explanation speaks for itself, as well as his humorous interpretation of the second movement, that quiet, tender soliloquy, as a " conversation "—even using a French word !—with the beloved. In the letter quoted above Beethoven thanks Moritz Lichnowsky for his efforts on behalf of the composer with the English Ambassador at the Congress of Vienna, Lord Castlereagh. Probably they were concerned with the production of " Wellington's Victory " in England. Here, then, lies the quite obvious motive for the dedication : the composer's feeling of gratitude.

CHAPTER XV

AFTER the Sonata Opus 90 Beethoven again allowed a couple of years to elapse before he sent out any new sonata for piano. This was Opus 101 in A major, completed in 1816 and published in 1817. Then followed more continuously :

Opus 106, in B flat major, begun in 1817, finished in the beginning of 1819;

Opus 109, in E major, begun (at the earliest) in 1819, finished in 1821;

Opus 110, in A flat major, completed in December 1821, published in 1822;

Opus 111, in C minor, completed in January 1822, published in the spring of 1823.

The ideas for the two last sonatas were conceived at about the same time, and these were completed more rapidly than was usually the case with Beethoven's productions during these last years of his life. Contemporary with the above-mentioned sonatas was the work on the great " Mass," which occupied the composer from 1818 till 1822; but apart from this no great works except the sonatas were completed during this period.

These five " last sonatas " were found to be bizarre, grotesque, inaccessible, and even meaningless productions, not only by Beethoven's contemporaries, but by those who came long after his death. In that respect they shared the fate of the last quartets, even though they were perhaps never actually, like the latter, called " mad."

Earlier writers of monographs on the sonatas have therefore exercised a certain carefulness in dealing with the "last" ones. In their special studies A. B. Marx and Reinecke are both surprisingly brief in their mention of these great works for piano. One does not wonder, though, that these writers recoiled from the well-nigh insurmountable task of conveying in words an impression of the subject and character of these strange and sublime works. The fact may have been that Beethoven had advanced so far beyond his time in them that more than a generation was needed before the musical world was in a position to understand them at all. Still more it may have been that executant musicians for some time gave these sonatas a wide berth, or, so far as one can see, if they did attempt to have anything to do with them, it was because it gave them occasion to display a superabundance of technical and physical ability, rather than because they wished to attempt any interpretation of them, which was also probably beyond their powers. On the other hand, the difficulties of the sonatas as a rule excluded them from the repertory of amateurs and of music in the home.

The first to perform in public the greatest of them all, the B flat major sonata, is said to have been Mortier de Fontaine, a Russian by birth, and Clara Schumann, but Hans von Bülow has perhaps been most active in making these sonatas known to a greater public, because of his intelligent interpretation, united to a fanatical enthusiasm, which he has also shown in the work of editing them. At the present day, as we know, they belong to the repertory of all pianists of any consequence, and they have put their predecessors in the shade to an extent that is almost regrettable. Moreover, the musical world is now no longer intent on their technical difficulties, but on their musical beauty and their artistic and psychological peculiarities, while later authors have devoted a detailed study to them, and endeavoured to elucidate their subject and uncover their depths—so far as this is humanly possible.

UNVEILING THE BEETHOVEN MONUMENT AT
BONN, 1845.

BEETHOVEN'S GRAND PIANO IN THE
" SCHWARZSPANIERHAUS."

The five sonatas are the chief outcome of the work of six years, and of these the period from 1819–21 was in a certain degree a pause. This is a perceptible decline in the productive power of the Master—hardly one piano sonata a year! And then Beethoven was never a rapid writer. But the conditions of his life were really growing sadder and sadder, more and more depressing and hampering, so that, as indicated before, his desire and ability to create necessarily suffered.

During these years Beethoven entered into the realm of total deafness. In spite of all kinds of " contrivances," no one could any longer make himself heard by him; communication with him could only be achieved by writing, by means of the " conversation-books," most of which have been preserved. And then his music ! We are told that once when Beethoven had given a very fine rendering of the sonata Opus 101 to a circle of friends, he declared afterwards that he had not heard *one note* of his own playing. This was in 1822, the same year in which Beethoven had to be removed with considerate care from the post of conductor at a rehearsal of " Fidelio," " a stroke of fate from which he really never quite recovered."

He was again, then—and now not only of his own free will—shut out entirely and irrevocably from communion with his fellow-men. He became more than ever a solitary, and felt it with pain—" what it is to be deprived of attention, of everything, of friends, and to be left to oneself; one must have felt it to realise what it means," he writes. He had also the bitter experience of being forgotten in his loneliness by those who before had applauded him. At the very time when these sonatas were being composed, the *Allgemeine Musikzeitung* states with forbearing indifference that " Beethoven is engaged in writing out Scotch songs, like Father Haydn at one time ; he seems to have grown too blunted for greater works." The small circle that still looked up to him and which he met daily did not, spiritually, reach to his shoulders. Letters and the conversation-books show how arid and commonplace was the atmosphere in which Beethoven lived with these closest friends. His personal affairs, his health, his works considered from the commercial point of view, these are the subjects of conversation; scarcely anyone cares to hear anything about his ideas, or shows any appreciation of his aims or of the subject and meaning of his works, and he therefore " hardly ever goes out, as it has always been impossible for him to associate with people when there was not a certain exchange of ideas."

But to the intimate circle, and still more perhaps when a stranger paid him a visit—as one of the " sights " of Vienna !— he could " sputter out gall and wormwood." . . . " He has a spite against everything, is dissatisfied and swears at Austria especially and still more at Vienna." This great solitary is the creator of the last sonatas. Physically shattered in health, indifferent to the claims or needs of the crowd, with an indomitable imagination, soaring at times to regions beyond human limitations, he reminds one of Rembrandt during his last days. One feels tempted sometimes to compare the Beethoven of these last sonatas with Rembrandt's last portraits of himself, in which there is a strange and awful grandeur, a new and impressive beauty. Violent, explosive in his artistic form of expression, he hurls forth his ideas in inspired sketches rather than in complete elaboration—and, as it seems to us, without any thought of what mankind will understand of his productions or what it will think of them.

It was not only deafness that hampered Beethoven because it excluded him from human intercourse. Continual illnesses also had a share in this. The unhappy artist, who doubtless also suffered greatly from his nerves, and felt the need of keeping hold of the few who were sympathetic and helpful, perhaps exaggerated his physical misery at times; but it is unlikely that Beethoven ever felt entirely well again and independent of physical conditions.

He was really ill again and again; jaundice, " a disease
that is so repulsive to me," rheumatism, diseased eyes and
gastritis harassed him frequently and often long, even before
the fatal cirrhosis of the liver broke out, followed by the distressing and ominous dropsy. A great deal of the desire to
work and of time would necessarily be lost, and even though he
might have the inclination, his physical state made it impossible.
Beethoven himself felt it deeply.   Well-known are the words
he uttered (during these years) : " I sit and think and think ;
I have had it in my head a long time, but cannot get it on to the
paper." Every creative artist is probably acquainted with
hindrances of this kind, but rarely has anyone " had in his
head " ideas so new and so difficult to convey as Beethoven at
this period. This *lingering meditation* which these words
reveal can be traced in more than one passage in the sonatas in
a very impressive way.

It is touching now to see how Beethoven, tormented as he
was by illness and made suspicious by deafness, still preserved
a certain ethical anxiety lest his trials should drag him down
to a lower moral level. In Shakespeare's *Othello* he underlined Desdemona's simple and beautiful words : " Heaven me
such uses send, not to pick bad from bad, but by bad mend."
From such noble and exalted feelings have his last works received
their stamp.

The " bad " surrounded him in several forms which can be
only briefly mentioned here.

First and chief among them were the relations with his
nephew, the son of his brother Carl. After this brother's
death, which in itself had a very depressing effect on Beethoven's
mind and on his production (see letter of February 28, 1816),
he had to engage in harassing lawsuits with his nephew's
mother, the " Queen of the Night," as Beethoven called her,
and later on, when his guardianship of his nephew was
acknowledged, the latter caused him many anxieties. The

biographies of Beethoven contain accounts of these endless legal contentions, which robbed the Master of his time and thoughts. One sees in these accounts how he felt his guardianship to be a mission, a sacred *duty :* " You must look upon Carl as your own child, and pay no attention to trifles, as compared with this sacred object "; finally one may read of the deep disappointments and sorrows that this charge was to bring him.

Next, there was his fear and struggle for the means of living : his quarrels and contentions with publishers, and his transactions which, with greater or lesser reason, have been placed in a light unfavourable to him. No doubt his suspicion and his ailing health had some share in this, yet, although a soberminded biographer may supply every proof that Beethoven's anxiety was unfounded, his complaining unjustified, as he was neither then suffering want nor had any immediate prospect of destitution, he could not himself reason calmly about it. Deprived of the most important of his senses, weakened physically and consequently also to a certain extent restricted in his ability to work, the future would seem very precarious to him ; and now as a " father " he was working not only for himself. Here, and not here alone, one feels tempted to speak in defence of Beethoven against his biographers.

Finally, the last worry and disappointment : the shipwreck of his hopes in regard to the arrangement of his home and household. It was just for the sake of the nephew Carl that he wished to exchange his restless Bohemian way of living for a settled and orderly home. But what a failure it all is for the unpractical, suspicious and close-handed artist ! For months, in fact for years, one can read in his letters, especially in those to his faithful and lovable friend, Nanette Streicher, wife of the piano manufacturer, about trifling matters concerning his rooms, housekeeping, prices of food and drink, washing and linen, the loan of a teaspoon, repair of shoes—and first and last about

NANETTE STREICHER.

DOROTHEA VON ERTMANN.

servants ! On this particular class of human beings Beethoven had concentrated his hatred. Even though he may not have had any reason to love his servants, housekeepers or housemaids, it is incomprehensible that he would allow such domestic affairs to take up so much of his time and thought. Is it not conceivable that Beethoven's servants, directly or indirectly, with or without reason, have deprived the world of more than one poem in music ?

In any case, however piteous is this back-stairs view of genius : these conditions and the state of mind which they created cannot be ignored, as they hampered his productive power and explain his need to find relief in art and an entrance to another, better and purer world than that in which he was doomed to live, whether this was due to his own fault or not. His works often contain evidence that his spirit was groping for such a rarefied, incorporeal dream-world which his imagination built up and endowed with a strange impalpable beauty.

His mind turns with longing and bitterness to the thought of death : he writes to Zmeskall (*vide* p. 36) (in August 1817) that he " considers himself doomed " (*i.e.* incurable), and in the true Beethoven manner he adds : " Thank God, I shall soon have reached the end of my part in the play ! " Another letter contains the words : " I am getting on better, though during last night I often thought of my death; still, such thoughts visit me in the daytime too." Even when he is speaking of his household, the words " upon which I have no hold, and which is most like an *allegro di confusione*," a grotesquely humorous exclamation reveals the world that occupied his mind : " The new cook looked sulky when she had to carry up firewood; I hope she will remember that Our Redeemer had to drag His cross up to Calvary ! "

In his loneliness, his broken health, his fear and his helplessness he often turns now in an odd, bizarre way to the " Providence " forming the core of his religious faith. " May

God help me; I appeal to Him as the highest instance."
(The continual lawsuits during these years must surely have
inspired this turn of expression !)   " Your state " (Beethoven's
own) " is hard enough—yet there is One above, He exists, and
without Him nothing exists."   " God, God, my protector, my
rock ! Oh, Thou my all; Thou seest my heart—oh, hear,
Thou ever unutterable, hear me, Thy unhappy one, unhappiest
among mortal men."   These few examples will suffice to give
an impression of where the Master sought refuge from everyday
petty worries and trials.   At this time he was at work on his
great Mass, and we have it from Schindler that he was in a
state of entire abstraction from the material world (" Erdenent-
rückheit ").   These moods, these notes from another world,
would be echoed in other works, and so we find more than once
in the sonatas that strange and visionary, indeed that " transfigured " expression, in which his genius, stirred by religious
emotion, finds an outlet for its feelings and its unconscious,
deeply philosophical contemplation.   It is like meeting the
Master in those holy places in which one involuntarily puts off
one's shoes !   Movements like the F sharp minor *Adagio* in
Opus 106, the variations in Opus 109, and in particular those
in Opus 111 have with good reason been called " revelations
from another and a higher world."—It was in 1820 that Beethoven wrote in his sketch-book the famous lines about his deep
admiration of the " starry heavens above our head and the
moral law within our breast," in order to fix in his memory a
very similar passage in Kant's *Kritik der Urtheilskraft*.*   Beethoven must have written movements in his sonatas like those
mentioned above, with feelings akin to those roused in him by
the splendour of the trembling and scintillating lights of the
heavens on a night of early autumn.

In music so spiritual there was no room for the broad and
often drastic Rhineland humour, so often met with in the
earlier sonatas.   As it grew rarer in his daily life, so it gradually

* Translated under the title, *Kritik of Judgment*.—TR.

disappeared also from his art. If we do encounter instances of humour now and then in the last sonatas, it is of a more delicate and playful kind, and on a lofty and ineffably higher plane, such as one also finds in Shakespeare towards the close of his life's work. The boisterous laugh, the biting mockery is gone, and the very name of *scherzo* occurs only once in the five sonatas.

The change, not only in the spirit of the music, but also in the style and language of these last works, was one of which Beethoven was fully conscious. There are several proofs of this from his lips or his pen, among the latter being this deeply resigned entry in his diary in 1816: "Opern und alles sein lassen—*nur für deine Weise schreiben*—und dann die Kutte, womit du dies unglückliche Leben beschliessest." *

The changes in style in the last sonatas are, of course, chiefly the same that we meet with in Beethoven's other works of the last period in the field of absolute music. It is outside the scope of this book to dwell further upon them, beyond what is entailed by the mention of an individual sonata.

Meanwhile, as a more personal element, the question has been touched upon as to whether Beethoven's total deafness may be considered to have affected his last mode of expression at the piano, and it is therefore particularly concerned with the piano sonatas. In earlier times especially this question was much discussed. Nowadays this feature is generally considered to be of minor importance, and no doubt this view is the right one. Certain peculiarities of style, such as that of placing the melody and the bass as far from each other as possible, without any part to fill up and bridge over the intervening space, might possibly with some reason be ascribed to the lost sense of hearing, on the supposition that Beethoven had forgotten the tone-effect of this pattern of notes, or had imagined other effects than the piano was

* Leave operas and all that alone—write only in your own way—and then for the monk's habit in which you will leave this unhappy life.—Tr.

able to produce. Other writers have maintained, however, that the extended positions and the empty gulf, as it were, between the voices, is a deliberate expression of something exalted, floating above the earth and having no root in the world of matter, and this view cannot altogether be rejected. In these sonatas we encounter bolder harmonic and modulatory effects than in the earlier ones, and these singular ventures can hardly be ascribed to deafness. To choose a small example, taken at hazard, the *Scherzo* of Opus 106 contains the following, as the solution of the leading *motif* :

but, when the same movement is repeated—after the B flat minor passage—and sounds essentially different (although the melodic part is unchanged) :

one may wonder at the oddity, the brusqueness or the obstinacy in the change, but hardly anyone with a little knowledge of the Beethoven of the third period will think the alteration is due to his lost sense of hearing.

CHAPTER XVI

The sonata Opus 101 in A major was composed at about the same time as the violoncello sonata Opus 102, which Beethoven defined as a " freye sonate " in his sketch-book. The same definition might be applied to the A major sonata. It is " free " in a manner resembling that of the two *quasi-fantasia* sonatas Opus 27, as not only its subject but its exterior form was decided by the composer's imagination much more than by tradition. It is true that the sonata has been called a work of transition, in so far as the traditional three parts are still present in their usual order, but regarded as a whole the sonata belongs to Beethoven's last piano style. Such as the first movement, in which the composer quite gives himself up to his emotional mood, and sings a beautiful, gently mournful song, which, despite the *Allegretto* heading, affects the mind mostly like an undulating *Andante*, and in which the decisive factor is the singing speech of all the voices, stirring the feelings of the listener, as in the first movement of Opus 27, No. 2, while the traditional modulatory section does not perceptibly appear. Beethoven himself did, in fact, call the movement : " träumerische Empfindungen," * and with delicate perception Nohl points out that an entry in the Master's diary at this time runs as follows (it may be a quotation) : " When a swelling tear is lurking under the heavy eyelids, restrain it with a firm will from gushing forth." This stream of tears, on the point of breaking out, and checked by force, is the feature of a mood which was soon after to be a favourite one with the romantic

* Visionary moods.—Tr.

school. It is not accidental, then, that Mendelssohn's melodies and Schumann's form of expression are foretold in this movement—in the hovering syncopes so full of forebodings; in the close which seems to fade away into ethereal regions; though the Master has a greater *control* of the emotional mood than any of his successors. The theme of the middle movement—which seems to be a brisk resolution after the too emotional one preceding it—is related to another of the romantics, Franz Schubert, who has caught it up in his G major quartette. It seems to be almost a jest that this movement is not called *Scherzo* but *Alla Marcia ;* this delicate and oddly moved piece is in any case not a march in the ordinary sense of the word. The term " march " can only indicate a certain precision and accentuation in the performance of the piece. It is an impressionistic piece of music, such as we often meet with in the last sonatas. It might suggest the phantasmal writings of Shakespeare's latest period, and Beethoven's strange exclamation (in a letter to Frederick Brunswick) is very appropriate to it : " My kingdom is in the air; the notes whirl as the winds stir them—so is the soul often in a whirl too." It will be noticed how the melody is thrown here in fragments, as it were, from part to part; it is the so-called " broken form " which is also characteristic of the style of the last quartets, and the doggedly carried out trio-canon with its false relations points in the same direction.

The *Adagio* introducing the last part is again an utterance of the feeling which Beethoven was pre-eminent in interpreting : that of longing. His heading above it, " sehnsuchtsvoll," is almost superfluous. There is no formal ending to the short but glorious section ; it flows out in a glittering coloratura which does not lead on to the *Finale* as one might have expected, but to a repetition of the leading subject of the first movement. It is a typical example of employing the reminiscent theme to link together the individual parts of the sonata, in a way peculiar to Beethoven's style during these last years, and found again in other sonatas and instrumental works. The composer now tears himself away from the gentle dwelling on memories, and resolutely attacks ("mit Entschlossenheit") the forceful, bright and bold final section, which is again characteristic in the fugated mode of writing frequently appearing in the last works, though in this instance it is combined with more lyrical parts. A scrap of melody, the folk-song character of which might remind one of the refrain in "The Dance on Riber Bridge" * turns up, but only in a casual form, without really being utilised. Is this accidental, or did Beethoven come across this tune in his study of folk-songs and repeat a few bars of it in his sonata, consciously or unconsciously? Riemann concludes his searching analysis of this sonata movement by declaring that in this instance the fugue part is a form of thematic work, executed in the service of fugal art. Anyhow, the movement is not a learned work, weighted by great scientific skill; on the contrary, it is a free and spontaneous piece of music, radiant with a bold, almost overweening sense of victory, and rising in interior and exterior power to close with a whimsical and graceful *Coda*.

The sonata was published in (February?) 1817; it had previously been performed by an amateur pianist, Stainer von Felsburg, Court secretary, at the concert of the violoncello player Linke on February 18, 1816, and Kalischer takes occasion to make the astonishing remark that it was the only one of Beethoven's sonatas to be performed *in public* during his lifetime.†

The sonata was announced as the first delivery of an "Anthology

---

* An old Danish folk-song. (Riber is pronounced Reeber.)—Tr.

† Thayer (Riemann) thinks that on the above-mentioned occasion it cannot have been the A major sonata discussed here, but the Opus 90, as that was then obtainable in print. This objection does not necessarily hold good, as the sonata (according to tradition) might have been played from the manuscript. Meanwhile Thayer himself is not clear with regard to this performance, as he speaks in one place about a first performance at Schuppanzigh's, in another at Linke's concert.

of Piano Music" started by the great firm of Stainer & Co.
In the original edition the sonata is furnished already on the
title-page with a description in French and German : on the
left "pour le pianoforte," on the right "für das Hammerklavier"
(Opus 106 is therefore not, as is so often stated, the first or
only sonata described by Beethoven himself as for the "Hammerklavier"). In a humorous letter, worded like a solemn
decree, Beethoven pronounces his resolve to introduce the
German designation of the piano. "Wir haben nach eigener
Prüfung und nach Anhörung unsers Conseils beschlossen und
beschliessen, dass hinfüro auf allen unseren Werken, wozu
der Titel Deutsch, statt Pianoforte *Hammerclavier* gesetzt
werde, wo nach sich alle die es betrifft so gleich zurichten und
ins Werk zubringen haben—*Statt Pianoforte Hammerclavier*—
womit es sein Abkommen einmal für allemal hiermit hat.
Gegeben, etc., etc., am 23. Jänner 1817." *

In the sonata there are also bilingual directions for *tempi*
and expression, but here they are in German and *Italian*.
On this point Beethoven evidently wavers. It was the desire
of his heart to get away from the Italian terms; he ventured
on it in Opus 90; in Opus 101 he shrinks from the consistent
point of view, as he is afraid that the German ones used alone
will have an unfortunate effect, either on the performers'
understanding, bound as they are by tradition, or on the
purchasers' reception of the work. In Opus 106 he returns
to German for the headings, but again uses the familiar Italian
for the indications of *tempo*—and this is about the end of the
struggle against the latter. It will be noticed how the German
headings in Opus 101 not only supplement but enlarge the
Italian ones, as if they were intended to speak more distinctly

* After due consideration and after hearing the advice of our Counsel we have
decided that from henceforth on all our works the German term Hammerklavier
shall be used instead of Pianoforte, and this is to be adopted and carried into effect
by all who are therewith concerned—instead of Pianoforte, Hammerklavier—this
pronouncement being hereby made once for all. Given, etc., etc., 23rd January,
1817.—Tr.

and earnestly to the Master's compatriots. Thus the first movement has the addition : *mit der innigsten Empfindung*, to which there is no corresponding direction in the Italian heading ; in the succeeding movements the directions are about synonymous, but in the *Finale*—as alluded to earlier—only the German language is used in a decisive place, in which we find the words : " Geschwind, doch nicht zu sehr und mit Entschlossenheit."

It is not unreasonable to suppose that these efforts of Beethoven to introduce a German music language may have influenced Robert Schumann, who employed German in his early works to an extent not previously known and with several bold turns of expression.

One dwells on the dedication of this sonata with peculiar interest. The Master bestowed this work upon Dorothea von Ertmann. She was one of Beethoven's most gifted and enthusiastic pupils, and assuredly one of those who understood his music most intimately and had acquired his way of performing it. She had a great reputation as an amateur pianist. Reichardt writes of her in *Vertraute Briefe :* * " I have never seen, even in the greatest virtuosi, such power allied to the tenderest delicacy ; there is a singing soul in each finger-tip." Baroness von Ertmann was *née* Graumann and belonged to a patrician family of Frankfort. After her marriage with the Baron, who was an officer in the army, she came to Vienna and there quite accidentally made Beethoven's acquaintance one day at Haslinger's, the music-dealer's, where she was just then asking for some of the piano music by the new Bonn virtuoso. She took it to a piano standing in the shop and began to play some of it. To her surprise a young man came forward from a corner, and seizing her hand thanked her warmly and with emotion. This was Beethoven. How highly he continued to value her and her musical gifts is shown by his after-

* Confidential Letters.—Tʀ.

wards always calling her his Dorothea-*Cecilia*, and by often asking her to perform his sonatas. According to the custom of the time she could not, as an officer's wife, play them in public ! Of her worth as an interpreter of Beethoven's music for piano Schindler says : " She alone was a conservatoire; except for Frau von Ertmann, Beethoven's music for piano would have disappeared still earlier from the Vienna repertory."

As so often happened to Beethoven's friendships, his relations with this beautiful and gifted woman seem to have had their ebb and flow; it is hardly possible to interpret otherwise the letter sent by the Master with the A major sonata :

" My dear, treasured Dorothea-Cecilia,—You have often been compelled to misjudge me, because I seemed to be what you disliked ; a great deal was due to circumstances, especially at an earlier time when my manners were less understood than now. . . . Please accept that which has often been intended for you as a token of my appreciation of your artistic talent and my affection for yourself personally."

It appears from a letter to the publisher, however, that Beethoven only decided on the dedication when the sonata had been put into the press. Meanwhile, if it arrived too late it seems that it was his intention to connect Dorothea Ertmann's name with a subsequent sonata for piano.

For some time Beethoven was a daily guest in the home of his artistic friend. She has related of him that he was very irritable, hot-tempered and sensitive, and therefore often unjust and suspicious even of his best friends, but this she attributes to his physical and moral sufferings, and for the sake of these everything was forgiven him. With a sense of humour her husband remembers Beethoven's habit of using the candle-snuffers as a toothpick ! But Frau Ertmann has also preserved

the touching account of how Beethoven, when she had lost a
dearly-loved child, to her surprise stayed away from her house
a long time and did not show his sympathy in other ways,
until he came back one day, weeks after. " He bowed to me
in silence, and sitting down to the piano he improvised on it
for a long time. Who would be able to describe this music ?
It was like hearing angelic choirs singing the welcome of my
poor child into the world of light. When he had finished
playing, he pressed my hand in sympathy and left me, silently
as he had come. He had told me everything and in the end
he brought me comfort," Frau Ertmann concludes, in the
account that she gave Felix Mendelssohn of this incident. For
as a young man Mendelssohn visited Frau Dorothea at Milan,
where the General was then garrisoned. In one of his vivacious
letters home he told his family about this visit : " . . . on
every hand I had heard accounts of how good and beautiful
this lady was ; how kind, how she had petted Beethoven, and
how beautifully she played--and the next day at two o'clock
I made the acquaintance of ' Freifrau Dorothea von Ertmann.'
She at once played Beethoven's C sharp minor sonata to me,
and afterwards that in D minor. She plays Beethoven's things
beautifully, although she has not practised them for a long time.
She often exaggerates the expression a little, retards too much
or hurries on again " (this gives one the impression that perhaps
Frau E. slightly exaggerated Beethoven's own manner of
playing, which she would have heard), " yet, on the other hand,
she played some pieces most wonderfully, and I think I have
learnt something from her. Sometimes, when she cannot
get more expression out of the notes, she begins to sing, in a
voice that seems to come from the depths of her heart."
(Here again there seems to be a suggestion of an involuntary
imitation of Beethoven's manner at the piano.) " Towards
the end of the *Adagio* in the B flat major trio (which the young
musician had to play to the ageing couple) she cried : ' That

place cannot be played at all for sheer expression ! ' and this is really true of the place in question."

As in the case of Opus 81 the dedication is an aid in explaining and understanding the next sonata work, the great B flat major sonata, Opus 106. Like the " Lebewohl " sonata it is dedicated to the Archduke Rudolph.

The sonata is one of the most famous and most denounced of them all; it is, so to speak, " the great beast " among the last sonatas. In its exterior form it is the largest in the series, a colossus in compass and subject ; it has, in fact, been called a " symphony for piano." * It belongs to the concert sonatas not only because of its ample four-movement stature, but also because of the splendour and power demanded for its performance. It is altogether on concert scale, notwithstanding the intimate and profound character of the *Adagio* and the difficulty of approach of the final movement.

Wonderful are the contrasts contained in this work ! The dedication explains the brilliance and festive splendour of the first part. The sketch-book contains a note on it adjoining a melody for a " Vivat Rudolphus," which seems to be very like the leading theme of the *Allegro*. This looks as though Beethoven, who, as related earlier, still owed the Archduke a " Mass," had wished to satisfy him—and his own conscience !— by working with might and main at completing another work in honour of the Archduke's birthday on April 17. This sonata, therefore, begins with an emphatic and festive flourish ; the opening theme sounds like a majestic and rousing *Vivat*, which establishes the main character of the sonata, and, later, the same subject is the foundation of the *Fugato*. But Beethoven soon abandons the personal point of issue, still more than in the " Lebewohl " sonata, and becomes absorbed in his own

* This agrees with the remark of Hans von Bülow, that the sonata requires a concert grand piano, one that can, so to speak, replace an orchestra.

deep contemplations—in the wondrous beauty of the second subject, hovering between major and minor ; he already seems to have left the Archduke and his birthday far behind, and soon, as so often before, he yields to his predilection for the fugated style, which he develops to the utmost of his powers. The movement becomes more and more stamped by the hand of the Titan of music ; it swells to thundering power in dissonant chords, unheard of at that time, and its tremendous rhythmic strength, its rich variety are displayed without restraint and in all their grandeur.

At the end of the movement, as in the first part of the " Lebewohl " sonata, a certain yielding and resignation are perhaps perceptible, as though the Master, after this violent display of the will to live, asks himself whether life is worth the struggle, until by main force he writes that *ff* close which recalls the festive origin of the sonata. In view of the amplitude and splendour of this work, demanding of a piano all that this instrument could give, the full and mighty chords, the whole bravura of the concert style, there is reason to remember that just when Beethoven was engaged on this *Allegro*, he received as a gift from the firm of Broadwood in London a magnificent, full-compass and fine-toned grand piano. Although the poor Master was totally deaf, one may surely be allowed here to speak of the interaction between inspiration and the exterior means of effect indicated in the mention of Opus 57.

The *Scherzo* of the sonata—the only one in the five " last "— is full of wit and grace, but also contains the rugged merriment now rare in Beethoven, and a few teasing riddles. It is a movement in which, to use the Master's own words, there are " whirlings like the wind," while the fantastic B flat minor belongs to those sections in the sonatas that foretell a later, impressionistic art in piano music. The composer seems to want to shake off the nocturnal hauntings of this section in the singular *Tremolo* (Temp [imo]) in order to return to the first gay and bright idea. Still, the demon is in him, he plays enharmonically with B flat and A sharp, slyly and playfully snatches at the remote key of B natural, until the movement closes with a delicate, hovering chord in B flat major (the sketch-book shows that he has been wandering round its uncertain " six-four " position, as though in careful search).

Despite all digressions from the *Vivat* attack in the first *Allegro* and from the straight *Scherzo* path in the second movement, the festive character of these two movements as part of a festive and congratulatory sonata are on the whole well maintained. Beethoven could therefore inform his distinguished pupil and friend that he intended to greet him on his birthday, the 17th April, with these two pieces. In May Beethoven went out to the country to Mödling, his frequent summer resort, and there applied himself energetically to the continuation of the sonata, the only larger work completed during that summer. During his country rambles, of which his favourite ones were in the lovely Brühler Thal, his ideas came to him and the work proceeded, as we can see from the sketch-book. While alone in these surroundings, communing with Nature and his own soul and occupied in the creation of his work, the occasion of the sonata recedes into the background ; the festive mood has passed and does not return.—The *Adagio* of the sonata becomes a prayer, its *Finale* an intellectual toil.

It is Nohl who has called the slow movement a prayer ; Lenz says that it is the greatest *Adagio* in the whole of musical literature. Both assertions hold good to this day, though perhaps not the latter in a literal sense. The beauty of this movement is unutterable, it cannot be translated into words ; it makes the highest demands on a pianist's technical ability, that does not allow one even to suspect the difficulties it contains ; it also requires the most exquisite sense of *timbre* ; for in this piece the deaf Master has charmed forth a *timbre* of wondrous

beauty, an inexhaustibly varied, sustained, singing quality that
was to be the model of much later music for piano, and demanding above all a humble-minded and tenderly sympathetic
absorption in the rare subject and essence of this music.
Reinecke says of this movement that even those who cannot
play the rest of the sonata should not omit to play this part.
Hans von Bülow for his part advises those who cannot fully
master this piece to leave it alone, because, as he says, all
mere *playing* stops here, and he who cannot " speak " on
the piano had better be content with " reading " the
music. Two different opinions and personalities are here
strangely at variance !—Beethoven himself has shown how
much importance he attaches to expression in performing it
by adding an *Appassionato e con molto sentimento* to the *tempo*
directions.

In this movement Beethoven's spirit seems to flee to a
world whither only the elect can follow it. H. Riemann, who
is not exactly lyrical, speaks here of " the holy of holies of the
temple of art." One involuntarily connects a movement like
this with something religious, such as that which has been
pointed out earlier, Beethoven's mind being stirred by religious
feeling during those years. But it is quite as certain that there
is something human in this music, human in the highest, purest
sense. A deep, gnawing pain finds utterance in the first chief
melody, introduced by those two notes, the tonic third and
fifth, which now seem to be so indispensable as the gate to the
Adagio, but which—according to the correspondence with
F. Ries in London—were not added at Beethoven's request
until at so late a stage that the sonata had already been put
into the press. There is a trembling, human hope of light
and happiness in the counter-melody in G major following
soon after, and introduced by that simple and wondrously
beautiful modulation, of which, as Riemann has pointed out,
there is a sort of forerunner in the sonata Opus 101.

Op. 101.

Op. 106

After this the movement consists of a sort of variations with rich, undulating figurations that raise the music up to higher regions of tone, in a delicate and transparent atmosphere, and seem to soften, though they cannot dispel, the sadness of the leading subject. A quite different tone position is needed before the full trust, confidence and peace of soul aspired to are reached. A new theme, of infinite simplicity and quiet nobility, is relegated to the deepest bass of the piano—this is perhaps the first time that the beautiful *piano* depth effect of the instrument is employed—and forms the basis of gentle, calm and not less simple movements in the treble. One feels that the Master has found, at any rate incidentally, the harmony and rest that he had been seeking. Is it possible to define a place like this by any other term than that of holy? Assuredly it has more than the tonality in common with a corresponding place in the *Adagio* of the ninth symphony (second subject). Yet we seem here to have met with a " still more ascetically exalted " (as Bülow calls it) musical expression than in the symphony.—Another comparison shows us two decisive stages on the long road of the piano sonatas, and so far they are connected with the goal aimed at in this description. It is that between this *Adagio* and that great *Largo* in D minor (Opus 10, No. 3), in which we contemplated the entirely spontaneous expression of the despair and suffering of the Master who was then still young, and these feelings were communicated in almost physically audible cries of pain. The *Adagio* in Opus 106 is the transfigured expression of the anguish and gentle renunciation of the Master's later years.

This mood of deliverance through resignation dominates the close of the sonata with the extended, seraphic tones of the F sharp major chords ; and Bülow observes with deep spiritual penetration that the leading subject, where it appears shortly before for the last time, in its original (minor) form although with fuller and more beautiful harmonies, should no longer express heartrending anguish, but a tearless surrender to fate.

In the sketch-book the following words are written beside the rough draft of this sonata : " auch könnte am Ende Rondo und Moderato und als Episode Fuge in B-Moll." The relations in this instance, then, are about the opposite of those in the quartet Opus 130. Owing to exterior influence, Beethoven in that case gave up the fugue movement, which afterwards appeared independently as " Grosse Fuge," while the quartet was given a more accommodating *Finale*. On his own initiative Beethoven here prefers the great fugue to the " Rondo " *Finale*, most likely more manageable, which he had also contemplated. Yet in spite of great admiration of the enormous labour, the imposing ability and strength of will in this *Fugue-Finale*, posterity has been somewhat reluctant to thank him for it. A musician like Reinecke writes that " he will not quarrel with anyone who is unable to find that this *Finale* is beautiful," and, to mention a quite modern composer, whose favourite style is this very contrapuntal one, Max Reger has incidentally called this sonata movement—a monster ! There is no doubt that it is the result of immense brain work rather than of spontaneous inspiration. It is significant in this connection that, before coming to the working-out of the *Finale*, the sketch-books contain studies of all kinds of ingenuities in the art of counterpoint and fugue. Before undertaking such a task even a Beethoven had to practise mind and hand in forms which, it can hardly be disputed, were not very closely bound up with his emotional life or his mode of expression. When Beethoven frequently returns to the fugue during this period, it seems to have been due rather to an act of will than to a desire of the heart. He has said himself, and of course with every right to do so, that " a fugue is an easy matter." But he could scarcely be unaware that it was a standing maxim amongst the musical " grammarians and their crowd " in Vienna that Beethoven could not write a fugue. One may therefore be permitted to think that, as a factor explaining the psychology of his motive, a certain spirit of defiance prompted him to show that he *could* write a fugue, and, moreover, a fugue that ventured upon and solved all sorts of difficulties, combinations and ingenuities—a fugue that could show both tooth and claw and in which no one should be able to equal him. But Beethoven maintains, where he speaks of the older art of fugue-writing, that " imagination has its rights too," and that " a new poetic element " ought to be added to the traditional form. It is from these points of view that the present fugue ought to be considered ; as we know, it is not modelled on the traditional systematic code, Beethoven himself indicating this (perhaps also by way of excuse) by writing above it : *con alcune licenze*. Now, when the *Finale*, despite all the exercise of imagination and inventiveness, and the efforts at renewal, does not arouse the poetic feeling in the listener that Beethoven certainly must have expected, nor communicate the bright joy to be found in solving a technical problem of music (as, for instance, in a Bach fugue), this is perhaps because the Master, in his ardent joy of creating, did not consider the capacity of the instrument he was using. Neither the piano of Beethoven's time nor that of a later day, no matter how great the mastery exercised in handling it, would probably be capable of solving clearly and satisfactorily, for the listener, the problems which have been set it in this fugue. Even the musical subject gives one the impression of the almost painfully energetic labour of a mighty intelligence rather than that of the spontaneous joy of inspiration, and most minds will probably agree with Thayer's (Riemann's) general verdict : " As a polyphonic, that is, a movement in itself difficult of approach, we think it is too long, and the melodic attraction is too often driven into the background by the elaborate details, which are certainly full of art, but often far too dominated by intellect, sometimes to the detriment of beauty of tone. . . . The fugue was not the natural form of expression of his deep and singular personality. Though the Master's art and the energy of his musical thought be ever so clearly perceptible to us in this movement, we do not take leave of it with the feeling of exaltation and inner warmth produced by other movements of this period."

When Beethoven sent the manuscript of the sonata to Ries in London, where it was to be printed, he sent with it the oft-quoted words : " The sonata has been written under the most trying conditions, for it is hard to have to write almost for daily bread, and that is what I have come to." One is startled on reading these lines. They may be the outcome of Beethoven's morbidly exaggerated anxiety about ways and means, and are perhaps intended to awaken the sympathy of the English public, on which he was now more than ever reckoning (also with a view to a journey to London). Or they may have

been a huge irony at the contrast between the infinitely exalted
world in which his spirit was moving, and the material misery
afforded him by life and his fellow-men.　But in the same letter
he also says : " If the sonata is not suitable for London I
could send another one, or you could leave out the *Largo* and
begin at once at the Fugue in the last piece ; or, first piece,
Adagio, at the third *Scherzo* and *Largo* and *All° risoluto*.　I
leave it to you to arrange it as you think best."　Impossible
to understand that Beethoven could with such directions—and
those not quite clear—in reality give a stranger *carte blanche*
about his work !

For he knew full well what it was worth and was quite clear
as to how and where it ought to be placed in his production.
When he answered an admirer, who at this time expressed his
enthusiasm over the Septet (Opus 20), that " I write better
things now ! " it sounds to our ears perhaps mostly like a
genuine Beethoven rejection, ironical, forbearing or con-
temptuous, of one who could *now* set up that old, tuneful
secular music as a model.　But when he *himself* calls the sonata
his " greatest," he can hardly have thought only of its exterior
size, and he writes to the publisher : " Here is a sonata for you
that will give the pianists something to do, and which will be
played fifty years hence."　A re-echo of Beethoven's oral
statement about the sonata may perhaps also be heard in
Artaria's advance announcement in the *Wiener Zeitung* of
September 15, 1819, which says : " In refraining from all the
usual laudations, which are, moreover, superfluous to all who
value Beethoven's exalted artistic talent, and thereby also
meeting the author's wishes, we wish to observe in but a few
lines, that this work is distinguished amongst all the other works
of this Master by the richest, greatest imagination, but that the
same, in respect of artistic perfection and set style, marks, as
it were, a new period in Beethoven's pianoforte works."

The Beethoven literature does not seem to contain much

about the contemporary reception of the sonata. Was it perhaps one of uncomprehending silence or of offence at being taken by surprise ? Nohl quotes some lines from the " Fischof manuscript," from which it appears that the novelty and " romanticism," as it would be called then, of the first two movements were to a certain degree understood. These movements are mentioned in such phrases as " the mighty creator of the world," and " the deep, creative freedom of the Master," while there is little understanding of the *Adagio*, and silence, apparently, about the *Fugue-Finale*.

CHAPTER XVII

During these (later) years of his life Beethoven once called the piano, till then the instrument he valued most, a "clavicymbalum miserabile." If not intended as a rough jest, it may have meant that his imagination was now engaged on such ideas and problems that the piano no longer satisfied him as a means for their expression. This may, as previously touched upon, have been the case with the *Finale* of the B flat sonata. He may also have meant that what he now had in his mind was not so much piano music as hitherto understood, as a song of the soul, having nothing to do with ordinary piano-playing. Even at the present day the variations in the E major and C minor sonatas suggest the thought that they are meant to be sung rather than played on the piano.—Meanwhile, before bidding farewell to his erstwhile favourite instrument, he bestows upon it three gifts, which fully prove his old love for the piano, and which, in contrast to the B flat sonata, are intimate and introspective.

These are the sonatas Opus 109 (E major), Opus 110 (A flat major) and Opus 111 (C minor), which, as the numbers show, followed each other in close succession, without other intermediate works, but otherwise so that only the two latter were written "straight off" a year after the first was published. In theme they are somewhat akin, especially Opus 109 and 110.

The sonata Opus 109 in E major is dedicated to Maximiliane Brentano, a young niece of the Bettina who for a time no doubt meant a great deal to Beethoven, as we have heard. She was the daughter of a Frankfort merchant, Franz Brentano, who with his wife, Antonie, *née* Birkenstock,

ANTONIE BRENTANO.

was an intimate and sympathetic friend of the composer, and
had helped him when he was in financial difficulties.
Maximiliane seems to have regarded Beethoven as a sort of
kind but somewhat eccentric uncle. The dedication of the
sonata would be intended chiefly as a compliment to her
parents, and most certainly cannot be interpreted as an indication of tender feelings for this quite young girl. It is more
likely that her mother had a warm place in Beethoven's heart,
yet only that of a friend. Frau Brentano was famed by all
who knew her, as one of the noblest and most interesting
members of their circle. Thus, her brother-in-law, the well-
known romantic author, Clemens Brentano, writes to her :
" For in you, my dear, the idol worship of our family, and
unfortunately also its mythology and its poetry, has found
its object." By good fortune the husband of this charming
woman was " the best man in the whole of Europe." At
the beginning of the nineteenth century these gifted and
lovable people moved to Vienna, where Beethoven became
their frequent and welcome guest. Frau Antonie was frail in
health and often refused to see visitors, but there is a story
reminding one of that told about Dorothea von Ertmann and
her dead child, in which we are told that Beethoven came, sat
down in the room next to that of his suffering friend and
played improvisations to her for a long time. When he had
told her all that he could in his own language and comforted
her he went out as quietly as he had come, without speaking
to anyone else in the house.

In the letter that Beethoven sent with the sonata he writes :

" To Maximiliane von Brentano—a dedication ! ! !

" Ah, well, it is not one of those that are misused by the
thousand. There is a spirit that unites all the best and noblest
people on this round earth, and which no age can disturb,
and that is the spirit now speaking to you and showing you

N

to me as it did in your childhood, as well as your splendid and gifted mother, and your good and kind-hearted father. Never will I lose the memory of people so lovable, and may you often think of me in kindness. . . ."

Beethoven's delicacy, often so beautifully expressed, is seen in the letter which he wrote at the same time to Maximiliane's father, and in which he says : " Without asking your leave, I made bold to dedicate a work of mine to your niece Maxe " (an odd slip of the pen for " daughter "). " Will you accept this as a token of my constant affection for you and all your family, and not misinterpret this dedication as in any sense a reward ? that would hurt me very much ; there are other and finer motives for such things, if one must look for motives. . . ."

Beethoven wrote to the publisher, Schlesinger (in Berlin), asking him to publish the sonata under the following title : " Sonate für das Hammerklavier verfasst und dem Fräulein Maximiliane Brentano gewidmet," and to add the year of publication, " such as I have often wished, but never has any publisher done so."

When the sonata appeared, at the end of 1821, neither this wish nor that about the German title had been respected !

The E major sonata is in three movements, of which only the middle one is fairly faithful to the traditional sonata form. The first movement begins : *Vivace, ma non troppo, sempre legato*, with a whimsical and charming theme, delicately touched with feeling, and undulating between the two hands ; a light and graceful, somewhat sprightly piece of music, which in regard to its dedication might well suggest the thought of an easily moved, buoyant and charming girlish mind. Yet in saying this it is by no means intended to suggest that there is any connection between the music and the dedication. Presently this tone gives way to lengthened arpeggio chords :

an *andante espressivo*, which, as so often happens in these
last sonatas, sings ethereal melodies on the higher notes; then
the *Vivace* reappears in the fantastic play of tone, to be interrupted anew by the *Adagio*. When the rapid part is heard
again, light, and as it were, more earthly, it is robbed of some
of its vivacity. A cantabile passage breaks into it, singing
out rest and peace, and in distant chords the music dies away
in a deep and closely placed *p* chord. (Bülow, not without
reason, added another *p*.) A writer thus interprets this passage :
" The world," that would call the master away from his work
on the Mass, is symbolised in the *Adagio* sections. For a
time the world prevails, but when the unearthly voice of the
Mass is heard again it seems to have overcome the world.
It is highly probable that the Master had some vision before
him when the theme of this music arose in his mind—we have
it on his own word that such was often the case—and the
varying character of the music assuredly contains a symbol.
But what is it? Perhaps the delicate and graceful *Vivace*
movement suggests rather a yearning after some feminine ideal,
but lacking the Master's own interpretation we are on uncertain ground.—The *Prestissimo* following it is also a lyrical
movement, but cast in a firmer mould. It soon becomes
evident that its introductory and leading theme, as has often
been pointed out, is closely related to the melodic form
for which Mendelssohn later showed great predilection. In
the case of Beethoven this melody is a rarity in its somewhat
strained and external passion, this mode of expressing passion
being foreign to him. Meanwhile it is interesting to see in
this instance, as in the sonata Opus 101, how the spirit of
romanticism finds utterance in these last works of the Master,
yet the majestic strides of the bass, which sustain the melody
and play their part throughout the movement, the solemn
secondary theme, the graceful passage and the inspired conclusion of the piece are altogether Beethoven.

After this section comes a *Finale*, soothing like oil on burning wounds. At the head of this movement, a theme with the variations so dear to Beethoven, there are, in addition to the usual instructions in the conventional Italian, further deeper and more intimate ones in German : *Gesangsvoll und mit innigster Empfindung*. It would be impossible for the piano to sing out this beautiful theme with enough purity and tenderness to satisfy him ! The noble simplicity of this melody makes it easily understood by everyone, while it must stir the feelings of all who have any ear for music. It moves on the simplest intervals, sustained by simple, natural harmonies, in its ineffable tenderness and depth of feeling it is somewhat like a folk-song. The melody is like a loving, sympathetic hand, gently stroking the head of a sufferer and giving relief where relief can be given. Involuntarily this thought suggests itself, when one remembers the dedication and Beethoven's endeavour to comfort his sick friend, Antonie Brentano, with his music.—In the first of the variations the composer soars up above earthly things, seeking ethereal regions in which the melody, in a slightly altered form, moves freely and independently, sustained only by the most necessary harmonies forming its accompaniment. The notes seem to beckon down a heavenly hope. In the next variations, in which the theme is, on the whole, easily perceptible, there is at times a charming gracefulness like that in the first movement, at others a bright gaiety, and again at other times the composer yields to his fancy for writing in fugue form, until in the last variation he again soars from the earth to where stars gleam and twinkle in long sparkling chains of trills. Yet *this* sonata was not to end in ethereal regions ; he leads it back with the unerring hand of a master to a more earthly and human close, and finishes with the consoling melody in its original form, with the unforgettably beautiful theme of the variations.

The next sonata, Opus 110 in A flat major, has been called
" a landscape sonata " (O. Bie), a description that sounds
clever, but which is scarcely more than that. Perhaps Nature
hardly ever spoke less distinctly in Beethoven's music nor
inspired him less than in these last sonatas. They express, in
a very high degree, like the quartets written soon after,
quite personal moods and states of soul. Even though the
glorious *Adagio* in Opus 106 may have come into being in the
composer's mind during his stay in the lovely Brühler valley,
the music tells us nothing about this source of its inspiration.
Nor is there the slightest indication in the A flat sonata that it
took form while Beethoven was staying at Döbling. There is
nothing descriptive or scenic to be found in this music. It
seems to be a purely spontaneous utterance of the feelings
that stirred Beethoven's heart and mind when he wrote it.
It is in a marked degree the music of a mood, and one may
venture to sum up that mood in the one word : *memories*.
There is about the whole of it something soft and transfigured—
as there is sometimes about memories ; at the same time,
because it is the utterance of a stricken man who feels the
advance of years, there is a tender melancholy, a plaintive
resignation at the sad " never more " ; at the bitter thought
that the past is irrevocably gone. Impulsive outbursts or
strong excitement, as in the sonatas nearest akin to this,
Opus 106 and 111, occur in only a slight degree. Even the
choice of key indicates a dreamy and emotional mood, and
Beethoven demands at the outset that the first movement be
played *cantabile* and *molto espressivo*—an insistence on expression
of frequent occurrence in the last works. The introductory
theme is furthermore to be played *con amabilità*, and the
significance of this should not be overlooked, in particular
because it is almost certainly only found in one other place in
Beethoven's piano music ; that is, in the " Bagatellen," written
at about the same period.

The very music of the movement also tends to show that it is not altogether a flight of fancy to talk of a " memory sonata." The melody coming after the beautiful introductory bars must have contained memories for Beethoven. Judging from its character it may have led his thoughts back to his youth, when the Mozartian cantilena was held in high favour, and the accompaniment itself is simple and old-fashioned, and as one might say, pre-Beethoven. Finally, there is the melody. Beethoven had sung it before in only slightly varied forms, and it now surges up again in his memory, to be clothed by him in its purest and simplest form:

Sonata Op. 10. No. 1.   1798

Violin sonata Op. 30. No. 3.   1802

Trio. Op. 70.   1808

Sonata. Op. 110.   1821

In the sonata the melody plays the part of one of those evanescent themes that fade away without any formal conclusion in arpeggiated chords, like mournful dreams.—The introductory theme only is used in the typically short modulation passage, and if one can be guided by Riemann's opinion on the subject, this again may have been a memory of the closing theme in the preceding E major, sonata.

The modulatory passage is in a parallel minor key reached by a single bold tone-gradation, and also seems to give voice to the disquiet and pain that memories may bring with them. The harsh dissonant harmonies, the restlessly moving bass-figures, though quickly yielding to a gentle transfigured calm, show, in an unexpected and threatening discord in the last bar but one of the movement, that the Master could not always " remember " without a drawn line of pain appearing about his lips.

The *Scherzo* that follows, as pointed out above, is the first F minor piece in the series of sonatas since the " Appassionata." Its leading theme is somewhat fierce, and is not an expression of Beethoven's gay humour, when he is on good terms with life, but, as a German interpreter rightly says, it is " grim and forbidding." *   The connection with the preceding movement is well preserved.   When other writers point out the likeness of the next theme with the tune of a popular ditty : " Ich bin liederlich, etc.," it is rather doubtful whether one ought to pay any attention to this resemblance as an instance of humour. Was Beethoven ever conscious of it himself ? Besides, it was no uncommon thing for the Viennese classical composers to make use of a popular theme in their instrumental music.   However this may have been, the brusque and

---

* " Was rauhes und grimmiges."—Tr.

jovial humour soon gives place to a queer and fantastic trio movement in which the humorous element is put to flight, while the delicately shaded memory dreams seem to float about the Master's head or to hover in his mind. The intangible, gossamer light passages on the higher notes of the piano, in which the left hand seems arbitrarily to sprinkle deeper notes like a frail and extended foundation, make no slight demand on the performer's art in expression and interpretation. It may well have inspired the piano music of young Robert Schumann. The surprising finish of the *Scherzo* in a major key—again a reversion to " old times "—is now felt to be the Master's retrospective gaze, gentle and tender, but free from pain.

The last section of the beautiful sonata—*finale* does not seem a fitting name for it—begins in an unusual way, like an orchestral introduction to a vocal scene, and soon a "recitative" is actually heard. It is a typical mode of expression in the last works. Its deeply moved, earnest " speaking " is immediately followed by a configuration which—again a reminiscence of earlier days—seems as though it would reproduce the languishing quiver (" Bebung ") so much in favour in the days of the old clavichords.* This introduction leads up to the beautiful *Arioso*, called by Beethoven himself *dolente*, for which he has chosen the remote key of A flat minor, as only once before in a sonata movement (Opus 26). An infinitely touching song, in its rising and falling cadences, in which the melody entirely predominates, the bass only sustaining and accompanying it, and closing with the seeming hopelessness of the *pp* octaves. After the last *Fermato* the mood changes ; the *tempo* to *allegro* (*non troppo*) and the pure homophony to strictly maintained polyphony. Once more the fugue becomes a spiritual fountain as a source of outlet for an emotion that

---

* In the 10th edition of Riemann's *Musical Dictionary* this interpretation of the figure is discounted.

threatened to become overpowering, but above this fugue Beethoven has not written any "*con alcuna lizence.*" Here, where he has not written, nor wished to write a traditional fugue, he has succeeded in doing justice to the poetic element. The theme and fugue are built up on simple, beautiful lines, on a noble, singing melody, as though the composer had in his mind the masterpieces of Bach, or perhaps rather of Händel. Yet the delicately branched-out work of this ingenious and poetic fugue does not give him rest for his soul. After the last *crescendo,* in which the theme is boomed out in bass octaves, a violent shake and arpeggio lead with the jerk of an abrupt interval of a second into G minor, in which key the *Arioso* is repeated and sounds gentler perhaps, but quite as charged with pain, and somehow duller in tone. Beethoven himself writes above it *perdendo la forza,* and the few changes now presented by the Arioso seem to reproduce restrained sighs of longing, not unlike the Quartet-Cavatina in E flat major with its "Beklemmt." Could it be that Beethoven was influenced by the trend to romanticism prevalent in the early years of the nineteenth century? In the intellectual world of Germany such men as Wackenroder, Novalis and Tieck came under its sway, and they are outstanding, highly strung and super-sensitive examples of this spirit, but the stupendous art of Beethoven could not be affected by it; his genius would break free as soon as it felt itself threatened by such a danger. It did so in this case. He soon abandons emotion and seeks for strength where he knows it can be found—in arduous intellectual work. The fugue reappears, but with an inverted theme, *in versione della Fuga.* Chantavoine would have it that this theme in this form is a forerunner of the "Es muss sein" *motif* in the quartet Opus 135, and therefore thinks it is significant in a way somewhat like that maintained above. The Master now elaborates the theme under various forms and according to all the ingenuities of the contrapuntal art, until first the three-part, and then the fugated style is abandoned, and the sonata is brought to a brilliant close with the same theme in full chords, in spite of all dissonances a victory over sad memories and haunting visions.

The A flat sonata appeared in Paris and Berlin at Schlesinger's. It carries no dedication, although it must have been the composer's intention to dedicate it to Frau Antonie Brentano, Maximiliane's mother. For unexplained reasons the sonata went forth without any name but that of Beethoven on the title-page. If it is to be regarded as a sonata of (the Master's) memories it is best so!

It is not quite clear whether there are any special reasons for the dedication of the next and last sonata, that in C minor, Opus 111. Beethoven left it to the publisher to decide to whom it was to be dedicated. He seems, after all, to have arrived at a decision himself, as he writes to the Archduke Rudolph, that since the Prince likes the new sonata so much, he will do himself the honour of dedicating it to him. Probably Beethoven and his publisher were agreed that it would be both right and fitting if this sonata, too, bore the name of the Master's royal pupil, for it did so when sent forth into the world. It was published in the spring of 1823 at Schlesinger's—" *tres respectueusement dediée à son altesse Impériale Monseigneur l'Archiduc Rodolphe, etc.*"

The form of dedication is probably that of Schlesinger rather than of Beethoven.

The sonata contains only two pieces, a *Maestoso* leading up to an *Allegro con brio ed appassionato* and an *Adagio molto semplice e cantabile*. In itself this two-movement form in a Beethoven sonata is not surprising, but interested contemporary musicians were astonished to find that the sonata finished with an *Adagio*. Could a sonata really finish with such a movement? Schindler questioned his Master and received the reply that " he had not had time to write a third movement." This answer has been eagerly seized upon as a fresh instance of Beethoven's drastic and half-contemptuous attitude to the puzzled inquirer, and once again Beethoven's humour has been a source of delight. Perhaps with some cause. But as Beethoven had actually sketched out an *Allegro Finale* and it is, moreover, a fact that the sonata was a sort of intermediate work, while the demands for the completion of the great *Mass* were continually becoming more pressing, it is quite possible that Beethoven briefly gave Schindler a simple piece of information without any hidden malice. It is true that this information leaves out the most important point, that is, that after the idea for this final movement had taken shape in his mind it would be quite clear to Beethoven that he did not need " time " for any other *Finale*. Not only was a *Finale* not required, but would have been antagonistic to the character of the sonata, already complete without it. Schindler was not alone, however, in his curiosity as to the absence of a *Finale ;* the publisher, too, was surprised at it, and distinctly nervous. First the younger Schlesinger writes from Paris that before proceeding with the printing of the new sonata, " which contains so many beauties, that only the great Master himself could have created it, I take the liberty of asking whether you have only written one *Maestoso* and one *Andante* for this work, or whether the *Allegro* has perhaps been left behind by mistake at the music copyist's." As Beethoven evidently did not think this lack of comprehension worth any answer, the elder Schlesinger himself wrote from Berlin : " In the present letter I only write to ask, with regard to the second sonata that you have sent me, and in which the second part is entitled *Arietta* (etc.), whether there is not to be a third and final part. I beg you urgently to send it to my son in Paris, addressed (etc.) or to inform him on the subject." It would have been rather amusing to have had Beethoven's answer to this inquiry, in addition to his reply to Schindler! One wonders whether Beethoven was not perhaps being somewhat supercilious in this silence towards the junior publisher.

The first part of this sonata has Beethoven's own heading of *appassionato*. This definition involuntarily takes one's thoughts back to Opus 57, and if you glance over the impassioned ones in the whole series, the sonata of youth in F minor (Opus 2, No. 3), especially its *Finale*, the work of manhood's years in the same key (Opus 57), and now this last sonata in the C minor key that meant so much to Beethoven, a comparison of both the spiritual and musical qualities will be well repaid and give a deep insight into the Master's changing manner and mode of expression.—The Beethoven of this *Appassionato allegro* is another than the composer of the gentle and ethereal A flat sonata. We have before us the Beethoven of the last years of his life—such as portrayed above. This was the man who, suffering deeply in soul and body, found no compassion or help in anyone; who, longing for peace and concord with his fellow-men, was met by indifference or ill-will. He it was, who wrote this " Maestoso " and " Allegro Appassionato." As a few years later he was to sit up on his death-bed, with his clenched fist raised high and threateningly, so, in his grand music-language he now clenches his hand and threatens the world and the destiny which allowed him to suffer without understanding him or bringing him comfort. At the beginning of his last sonata he hurls the lightning and thunder that were to attend the last hour of his life. The ascending chords of the *Maestoso*, which Beethoven perhaps never equalled elsewhere in power and conciseness—the glorious, strong and bold modulations, after the booming voices of storm in the bass, find an outlet, like " a volcanic fire," in that tremendous anathema, the three-

toned *motif*, petrifying like the wrathful gaze of a Titan.   Riemann has drawn a parallel between this theme and the chief
melody in Schubert's beautiful song of " Atlas," and the
resemblance is significant, because in both cases the composers
wished to express the revolt and defiance of a Titan, of gigantic
suffering, as in the words of Heine's poem, " Die ganze Welt
der Schmerzen muss ich tragen ! "

This leading theme *—Beethoven at first intended to use it
in a fugue, but with the keen insight of genius he gave up
this idea—really dominates the whole of the impassioned
first movement, in which the numerous directions as to tone-
shading, the frequent changes of *tempo* (and *retinente* and
similar directions) indicate the violent emotion that it
expresses.

The theme is continued in thundering octave-passages, and
as an accompanying theme it is given a kindred tone-figure,
which mostly contributes to increase the impassioned flight
of notes still further,

while a secondary theme, as so frequently occurs in the music
of this period, is indicated rather than carried out.   Its A flat
major need of opening its arms in the wild struggle to those
" who suffer and are heavy-laden " does not make headway.
After the huge leaps from the highest treble to the deep bass
preceding its appearance, it remains feeble and delicate, and its
gentle mood is soon torn asunder by the passionate *ff* passage
of discords sweeping down the whole length of the keyboard—
one is reminded of corresponding outbursts in Opus 57.   The

* Beethoven had noted it twenty years before his present use of it.

leading theme is again the ruling one in its harsh sternness, while the first part is brought to a close through hurrying semi-quaver passages with exciting *sforzati*.*

Following his first intention, and at this time his prevailing desire, the Master introduces a fugal part into the modulatory section. But, as though feeling the need of a freer mode of expression here, Beethoven soon gives up the fugal manner, and we witness, as in the case of the " Appassionata " sonata, his increasing excitement, caused by the exertions of his art, and the development of a passion continually growing in violence. The section that culminates with the main theme played in four unison octaves is in its scantiness one of the most pathetic and stately passages in the sonatas. It will be noticed, however, that the second theme, when it comes forward again (in C major), has acquired greater weight, as it were, and gained more room for itself : a harmonious ending to the movement is already presaged. But the impassioned leading theme is still predominant ; once more the crashing discords thunder down the whole length of the keyboard, and soon we perceive (in the comparatively short *coda*) how the Master intends with a great effort to calm the spirit torn by conflicting passions. The dissonant *sf* chords, gradually falling into *diminuendo* and significantly closing on the un-accented beat, are like a rider curbing his wild horse by sheer power and strength of will. There are still low rumblings in the bass, reminders of sufferings and struggles gone through, but the trembling discord, and its resolution into calm C major chords fading away to *pp*, testify to the calm that has been reached at last, and form the natural transition to the final movement of the sonata, which assuredly, as Hans von Bülow

---

* W. Nagel is probably right in saying that this first part should not be " repeated," in spite of Beethoven's directions; a music outburst so violent and as it were involuntary, and improvised in character, may lose rather than gain in interest by being immediately repeated. Besides, the plastic form of the main motive renders it easy to follow its treatment in the ensuing part.

would have it, ought to follow without almost any intervening pause.

A more beautiful close to Beethoven's sonata work than this *Adagio* cannot be imagined. It may accidentally have become the last stone in the monument of the world-famous series, yet one would like to think it significant that this pure, transfigured and exalted music was to be his last word as a sonata composer. A Danish author * once wrote that Beethoven, with an " odd, savage irony," called this piece an arietta. If there is any trace of irony in the choice of title— and who, in considering Beethoven's whole nature, will dare to deny it ?—then it must be a genius of irony that has risen above a world of good and evil, to the threshold of a purified region, and to heights from which it can contemplate all things earthly in diminutive form. But there is nothing " savage " to be found in this music. It is true that these variations were not written by one who was happy, in the ordinary commonplace sense of civic life, but by one who had come to terms with the world and himself—and who feels that he has conquered because he has attained to harmony.

Moreover, Beethoven's conception of the movement is made evident by his having added to the *Adagio : molto semplice e cantabile*, and once more it is seen that during these last years, simplicity of expression is his most frequent aim ; spiritually considered, the movement, together with the first part of the sonata, gives a picture of the Beethoven that the previous chapter essayed to describe, with the great irreconciled contrasts between embitterment, hate, defiance on the one side, and gentleness, self-chastening and religious surrender on the other.

This movement is *molto semplice* from the very beginning of the theme, which is somewhat in the direct style of a folksong. One learns with wonder that in its original form the

* Karl Gjellerup: *Der Dichter und Denker*, Dresden, 1921–22.

melody lacked the figure which gave it its natural grace and suppleness, and which further on means so much.

The variations are " very simple," in spite of their demands upon the technique, and still more on the deep understanding and humility of their interpreter. They were written by the Master after he had uttered his last word of doom to the world, and had retired to his own " transfigured " region, where he wrote only to satisfy himself. Often strange, impalpable notes, like those of dreams, are heard in these variations ; they are akin to the memory moods of the A flat sonata, but here the memories seem to have been caught up into a still purer region, rendering them more beautiful; and the last remnant of bitterness has vanished, together with every trace of the morbid sensitiveness of the time.

The theme is also simple from a harmonic point of view. C major predominates in it ; not until the second part does the delicate sombreness of A minor supervene. The variations follow just as simply in regard to key ; for a short space only room is given to the more remote E flat, but C major soon returns, and at length the A minor retreats so that the piece may close in the undimmed brightness of a clear and ringing C major.

Rhythmically considered, the variations are not so simple. On the contrary, they are called " an Anthem to Rhythm," and they certainly are a rhythmic anthem, brimful of inventiveness and imagination. Foremost among the classics the rhythmist has here once more displayed all his strength and beauty. It is therefore difficult to agree with Hans von Bülow in feeling a " Nirvana " mood in this music. Quite exteriorly one notices strange, uncommon time-beats, rarely or never

BEETHOVEN (*c.* 1823).
*(From a portrait by Robert Krauss after the original of Waldmüller
and the cast of his face.)*

before used, such as 9-16, 6-16, 12-32. This multiform
rhythm, which one admires in variation after variation, points
towards the future, as well as the Beethoven impressionistic
form of utterance, mentioned earlier, and evident in the
fourth variation, in which " the bass sounds like a misty, soft
and dull humming, like a distant sound of bells, with floating,
mystic chords borne by the wind, above them " ; with the
softness of night they seem to cover the notes of the melody
lying hidden in them. Everything is hinted at here, there
is a feeling of something ominous behind it. It is after this
variation that room is made for a moment for the key of E flat
and for a contrasting, mournfully accented short antiphon
between the treble and bass. But soon (in the last variation)
the melody rises on the wings of C major in high full notes,
above everything earthly, until (as in Opus 109), wreathed in
a chain of trills, it symbolises the joy of the Master at the
deliverance of his soul from all that would drag it down.
We seem again to gaze up at a vault of gleaming stars, and this
is the end of the last sonata movement. If, as it seemed for a
while, Beethoven had thought of concluding this *Adagio*
with the theme in its original form, we understand full well
that he could not have done so here, where he seems to
have risen above all things earthly ; where the marvellous
beauty of his world of music and the deep wisdom of his
thoughts have opened for us a view into a beautiful, mystic
and far-off land.

We have come to the end of our contemplation of Beethoven's
piano sonatas. Link by link we have gone through the long
chain of these beautiful tone-poems, completed one hundred
years ago. No music poet has ever been able to produce
their like, and it is doubtful whether the world of music will
ever see anything to compare with them. Every link in this

O

chain has taken form in the imagination of a genius, it has been modelled by the hand of an artist, and brought to perfection by his untiring perseverance. In the main this series of sonatas has remained unaffected by the passage of time. It contains some of the most valuable productions of the art of music, and even those which have remained less known, less often played, and which occupy a humbler place in the series, are of value and consequence, regarded in the light of the Master's personality and of the circumstances of his life, as it has been the aim of these studies to point out.

Beethoven's sonatas, as explained in the preface and in the first chapter, have here been considered from certain limited points of view. If those who wish to make a deeper study of the sonatas find that this little book is a useful and illuminating help towards understanding and performing these great musical works of art, then its object will have been achieved.

BIBLIOGRAPHY

Books to which reference has chiefly been made :

(i.)   Biographies of Beethoven; the most valuable is that by A. W. Thayer (Ludwig van Beethoven's Leben, 1866; edited, revised, and translated into English by H. E. Krehbiel, 1921) ; next those by A. F. Schindler (Biographie von Ludwig van Beethoven, 1840, 1845, 1909; translated into English, edited by J. Moscheles, 1841) ; L. Nohl (Beethoven's Leben, 1867; revised by P. Sakolowski, 1912; translated by J. J. Lalor, 1884, 1893; by Emily Hill, 1895); A. B. Marx (Ludwig van B., Leben und Schaffen, 1901) ; W. A. Thomas-San Galli (Ludwig van B., 1913) ; P. Bekker (Beethoven, 1911 ; translated by M. M. Bozman, 1925) ; J. Chantavoine (Beethoven, 1907) ; T. von Frimmel (B. und Goethe 1883 ; and Josef Danhauser und B., 1892) ; G. Ernest (Beethoven : Persönlichkeit, Leben und Schaffen, 1920).

(ii.)   Works dealing especially with the sonatas : by A. B. Marx (Anleitung zum Vortrag Beethovenscher Klavierwerke, 1875) ; C. H. C. Reinecke (Die Beethoven'schen Clavier-Sonaten, 1896, 1912 ; translated into English as the Beethoven Pianoforte Sonatas, 1898) ; E. von Elterlein (B.'s Pianoforte Sonatas, 1898); Wilibald Nagel (B. und seine Klaviersonaten, 1923, 1924); C. W. J. H. Riemann (L. van Beethovens sämtliche Klavier-Solosonaten, 1919).

(iii.)   Other works : Dr. A. C. Kalischer's Beethovens sämtliche Briefe, 1906–1909; trans. by J. S. Shedlock, 1909; F. G. Wegeler and F. Ries's Biographische Notizen über L. van B., 1838, 1906 ; T. von Frimmel's Beethoven-Studien, 1905 ; Dr. A. C. Kalischer's Beethovens Frauenkreis, 1910; F. Kerst's Die Erinnerungen an Beethoven, 1913.

(iv.)   Also less important books by L. Ritter von Köchel (Drei und achtzig . . . Original-Briefe, 1865) ; La Mara [pseudonym, i.e. Marie Lipsius] (Beethoven und die Brunsviks, 1920) ; Max Unger (Ludwig van Beethoven und seine Verleger, 1921) ; Conrad Huschke (Beethoven als Pianist und Dirigent, 1919) ; and others.

(v.)   Articles in periodicals, especially in the publications of the Internationale Musikgesellschaft and in Die Musik.

CONSPECTUS OF BEETHOVEN'S PIANOFORTE
SONATAS

INDEX

Names and Works (excluding Pianoforte Sonatas)

INDEX OF SONATAS